CONTENTS

ANNA-LUSE

David Mowat is one of the new British dramatic authors who has found a way of combining the contemporary pre-occupations of his generation with new theatrical techniques that employ surrealism, fantasy and free continuity, while at the same time writing in a way that is highly individual, very personal and, unlike most recent authors, authoritative with a sense of depth.

The three plays in this volume have been produced in Edinburgh, Manchester, London and Amsterdam, and part of ANNA-LUSE was filmed for French Television.

ANNA-LUSE was first performed at the Traverse Theatre in Edinburgh as a Festival production where it created a considerable sense of shock for its daring, as well as fascination for the craftsmanship with which it explored the mind of the protagonist, a young blind girl, who though innocent, is aware in her naivety of every contemporary situation and endowed with a natural erotic acceptance.

JENS, written a year earlier, was first presented at the University of Sussex and has since had further productions, all of which succeeded in exciting the audience with the way the author is able to call the changes in a given situation, equating the human with the animal in a play that uses symbolism as effectively as Strindberg in uncovering the inner personalities of the characters.

PURITY, first presented at the Stables Theatre Club, Manchester, is perhaps an easier play that investigates erotic fantasy with great courage but with a sense of tragedy that is surprising in an author who is only at the beginning of his career.

David Mowat is 26 years old, read English at New College, Oxford and spent two years doing research at the University of Sussex. Whilst there he also produced many plays by himself and others and in 1969 he spent a short time as resident writer with the Traverse Theatre Club.

OTHER C AND B PLAYSCRIPTS

* hardcover, + paperback

*All plays marked thus are represented for dramatic
presentation by C and B (Theatre) Limited,
18 Brewer Street, London W1R 4AS

PLAYSCRIPT 27

'anna-luse'
& other plays

JENS
PURITY

david mowat

CALDER AND BOYARS · LONDON

822
MOW

First published in Great Britain 1970
by Calder and Boyars Limited
18 Brewer Street, London W 1

ⓒ David Mowat   1970

SBN 7145 0643 5 Cloth edition
SBN 7145 0644 3 Paper edition

Printed in Great Britain
by The Pitman Press,
Bath, Somerset

ANNA-LUSE
1966

ANNA-LUSE was first presented at the Traverse Theatre, Edinburgh, on 17th August, 1968, with the following cast:

ANNÀ-LUSE	Pamela Farbrother
SOLVEIG	Sarah Kidd
JIRI	Anthony Haygarth
ROY	Derek O'Connor
JEAN	Angela Galbraith
INGA-LILL	Claris Erikson

The play was directed by Max Stafford-Clark

The play later transferred to the Mickery Theatre, Amsterdam, with the following changes in the cast:

SOLVEIG	Claris Erikson
JEAN	Della Matheson
INGA-LILL	Pamela Moiseiwitsch

Note: Anna-Luse and Solveig are blind
         Luse is pronounced 'Luce - r'

(ANNA-LUSE asleep in bed.
A minute elapses.
She begins to stir.
She sits up.
Some moments elapse.
She gets out of bed and sits on the side of it.
She gets up, takes a kettle and leaves.
A minute elapses.
She returns, pours water from the kettle into a bowl,
and washes and dries her face.
She enumerates objects in the room, and parts of her
body, touching the objects as they occur.)

ANNA. Table, bowl, kettle, soap, towel, wall, sheet,
pillow, floor. Foot, toes, calf, knee, thigh, genitals,
hips, navel, waist, ribs, chest, breast, nipple,
shoulder, finger, hand, arm, elbow, neck, chin,
mouth, nose, eyes, ears, hair.

(She performs one or two exercises, some on the
floor, some on the bed)

Anna-Luse. Foot, toe, calf, knee, thigh, genitals,
hip, navel, waist, ribs, chest, breast, nipple,
shoulder, finger, hand, arm, elbow, neck, chin,
mouth, nose, eyes, ears, hair.

(She goes behind a screen, and changes into a slip.
She reappears, finds a dress and puts it on. She
prepares some coffee, and sits on the bed drinking it.
SOLVEIG enters. She calls)

SOLVEIG. Luse. Anna-Luse.

ANNA. Solveig? Hello.

9

SOLVEIG. Anyone else here?

ANNA. Don't think there are.
Anyone: hello.

SOLVEIG. I thought you might have been asleep.

ANNA. I woke up.
Jiri?

SOLVEIG. What?

ANNA. Old fellow: sometimes falls asleep here.

SOLVEIG. Where would he be?

ANNA. Sofa.

(SOLVEIG makes her way over to the sofa)

SOLVEIG. No one there.

(She sits down)

ANNA. Give me a kiss.

SOLVEIG. Come on over here.

(ANNA-LUSE comes and sits on the sofa. SOLVEIG
gives her a kiss)

ANNA. Nice.

(Some moments elapse)

Would you like some coffee?

SOLVEIG. Is there some left?

(ANNA-LUSE gets up)

ANNA. Think so. Think there is.

(She goes over and fetches her mug. She gives it to

SOLVEIG)

SOLVEIG. Lovely. Not bad.

(She drinks it)

Shall I put the -

ANNA. I'll have - I'll take it.

SOLVEIG. There.

ANNA. Tell me about Sven. Something.

SOLVEIG. Who?

ANNA. That boy. What it was like.

SOLVEIG. What do you mean?

ANNA. Anything. Any detail. Anything.

SOLVEIG. I can't tell you anything unless I know what you
     want to -

ANNA. Anything you can think of -

SOLVEIG. Well, we -

ANNA. That comes into your mind.

SOLVEIG. We -

ANNA. Yes. Tell me.

SOLVEIG. I'll tell you something else. A teacher I had,
     recently: fairly recently. She didn't realise - : and
     wanted me to tell the difference between two
     sentences she'd written on the blackboard. I pretended
     I could read them, and made up an answer - something
     or other, and she thought, of course, I was teasing
     her, because I made up very peculiar sentences and
     compared those.

ANNA. When did she - When did she realise?

SOLVEIG. She came - After a bit she came over and
shook me. She really thought I was teasing her, she
really did. I know I shouldn't have done it, but I
thought it might be just as well to invent sentences. In
fact the ones she'd written were about cornfields and
the crops - you know - planted by farmers, that kind
of thing.

The ones I made up were quite different.

ANNA. When she knew: what did she do then?

SOLVEIG. Then, it was odd. She was very quiet. I can't
remember. She went out of the room.

ANNA. Were you alone?

SOLVEIG. She went out - came back again a few minutes
later - and she was very different. Yes, I was alone.

ANNA. I'm not sure that's fair. I don't think I'd do it.

SOLVEIG. I wouldn't usually. She was quite a nice
teacher: but some things - she just couldn't see them.
You know, you know, when we came to triangles I had
to take over: I had to teach her, because I didn't want
her teaching other people wrong. I had to teach her
about triangles. She was hopeless on them.

ANNA. I wouldn't do that.

SOLVEIG. What would you? Let her not know and have the
wrong idea, and teach other people the wrong things?

ANNA. Are you sure? About it being the wrong idea?

SOLVEIG. She didn't have a clue. She was quite nice. She
was - no, but she was telling me all the wrong things.
I laughed at her - almost - at one point.

I just had to teach her. I even drew some figures for
her on the blackboard.

I don't think - well - I'm not sure she was even certain how many sides a triangle had or whether they were closed or open at the top.

ANNA. I wouldn't have done that. I'd have pretended she was right.

SOLVEIG. I might - yes, but - the children, though - when she'd have taught children the whole wrong idea and they'd believed her.

ANNA. Are triangles open at the top?

SOLVEIG. Surely you know.

(JIRI enters)

JIRI. I - why: pardon me.

ANNA. It's Jiri.

SOLVEIG. Hello, Jiri.

JIRI. Why, -

ANNA. Hello, Jiri. Can you close the door and come in. Would you like your usual seat? We'll move over here.

(The girls vacate the sofa)

I want you to tell me about Sven. Please.

SOLVEIG. What?

ANNA. Tell me.

SOLVEIG. I - what d'you want to know?

JIRI. I may -

ANNA. What is it, Jiri?

JIRI. Anna - most pleased. It is Anna? Must confess, I -

ANNA. Anna-Luse.

JIRI. I was waiting to see one of the - ah - young men - Paul, I believe his name is.

ANNA. Roy.

JIRI. Though, I must admit - none too sure I've made the acquaintance of your young friend here.

ANNA. Her name's Solveig.

JIRI. I - ah -

SOLVEIG. Solveig.

JIRI. Why - must say, I'm impressed by some of these objects. New, aren't they?

ANNA. No. No, those were there last time.

JIRI. Attractive. A type of small briquette, I believe.

ANNA. He's - Whenever he comes he takes a fancy, you know, to little objects and things, and -

Don't put them all in your pocket, Jiri, please.

JIRI. Why - I was - I was comparing them, actually, trying them against the lining of my pocket. Very attractive colour.

ANNA. We know, Jiri. But leave some for us, please. Where's your magazine? Have you brought it with you? Ah - there: under your arm. Would you like to read it?

JIRI. Fond of these briquettes, too, are you? To tell the truth, Anna - Anna is the name, is it? - the young fellow supposed to be taking you - name of Paul - was in an encounter with some youths.

ANNA. What? Roy? Youths?

14

SOLVEIG. The person who's taking us, you mean?

JIRI. Roy: walking alone one of those narrow paths, I
fancy, he was encountered with a small party of youths
- three or four lads. A minor argument took place,
and Roy found himself in the water.

ANNA. Swimming?

JIRI. Pushed - propelled into the flood.

SOLVEIG. Do you think it's true?

ANNA. May have. His imagination's lively. Would you
like to sit down, Jiri? Rest. Read.

JIRI. Not - evidently - concerned with the fate of this
fellow.

ANNA. There. Comfortable. Got your magazine? Now
read it.

Please tell me about Sven. The others will come. The
others will be coming. I love you.

SOLVEIG. Sh.

ANNA. Tell me.

SOLVEIG. It was at one of those conferences. He played
an instrument - some instrument or other - and we had
bedrooms next to each other.

ANNA. What was he like?

SOLVEIG. Ordinary. Quite nice. He didn't usually say
very much.

JIRI. I beg your pardon: it's to Paul you're referring?
Caught a word, I confess.

SOLVEIG. No, it's not about Roy.

JIRI. Fell off the path, you know.

ANNA. Shocking.

JIRI. Of course, I don't know about the others. For me,
however, it was disconcerting.

(He rises)

I dare say, at times, you have felt -

ANNA. We're not. It's not about Roy. Could you - please
could you just read -

SOLVEIG. Where's he going?

ANNA. He's after another briquette. Jiri, we love you,
but please, please: your magazine's -

JIRI. Beg pardon?

ANNA. Your magazine's interesting, you know, and full
of - and full of nice stories - Pictures.

SOLVEIG. I can see a girl on a bicycle in that one.
Wearing only a -

JIRI. Solveig. I'm delighted. I can see you're also an
admirer of these objects.

ANNA. It's no good - he slips the things into his pocket
at once. I don't think he even notices.

JIRI. Certainly something to admire.

SOLVEIG. Then why not fish them out later?

JIRI. I wonder if you'd be prepared to part with - for a
price, naturally -

ANNA. It makes him very distraught. I've known him
argue for hours that a thing was his own.

SOLVEIG. And it wasn't?

ANNA. He'd taken it.

16

JIRI. Taken - uh - Anna: may I take for investigation -

ANNA. Take - can you take his other arm?

JIRI. I -

ANNA. Would you like to sit? Now - the magazine's there. You can read it, and we'll be here.

SOLVEIG. If you come across interesting bits as you're reading, you can read them - read them out to us.

JIRI. Why - a prospect of some substance. I'll just -

(He reads)

ANNA. Then? Yes.

SOLVEIG. We - we haa our food - sandwiches. Then we discovered a place inside, completely hidden: it would really have been the obvious place to have had the food, still, we had eaten it, we -

JIRI. Sumiuna atuarsinaussaunik angakok ukiup asimiokarfingme kalatdlit ilait umiarssuit.

(The girls talk privately)

Tassalso inungnik umiarssualivingmileriangualdlarlut okautigait agdlagkamik. Taimailissut ama ajulermagit nuvdlo maingmat. Ajordlutik katerssiput aitsat auatanut nunaliufigssacrugkamik kanigdliartoraluard- lutik amerdlauatdlarmata pujorssuardlo takordlornermik. Nuvdle sakunik.

ANNA. More, or less?

SOLVEIG. More.

ANNA. And afterwards?

SOLVEIG. (Inaudible)

ANNA. I wouldn't. I'd be scared.

17

SOLVEIG. After the... (inaudible)

ANNA. (Inaudible)

SOLVEIG. At the best moments you often feel nothing, and just think of it happening.

ANNA. And Sven?

SOLVEIG. (Inaudible)

JIRI. Originals, I believe. Why, very probably.

ANNA. I wouldn't want to have a baby. I'd be scared.

JIRI. A baby?

SOLVEIG. No. We're -

ANNA. It's just an improvisation we're preparing for Roy.

JIRI. Are you now? I - perhaps I might - may I participate perhaps?

ANNA. It's not really a -

SOLVEIG. It's not a thing that can be done with three. You see, we - If we don't, I mean if we're not good he'll have to get rid of us, and, you know, that'll be the end of everything.

JIRI. It's to Paul you're referring?

SOLVEIG. Roy.

JIRI. Why, the fellow was involved in some uncomfortable business, I understand.

(ROY enters. His clothes are wet)

ROY. Clean trousers?

ANNA. Roy. Hello.

JIRI. Disturbed by the event, Roy: glad you've extricated yourself: nasty tumble, that.

ROY. Saw it, did you?

SOLVEIG. Hello, Roy.

ROY. Too many of them - four or five. Rough chaps unluckily. Got one of them down: others did for me.

SOLVEIG. What happened?

JIRI. Feared, myself, you might have had more trouble.

SOLVEIG. What happened? Are you all right, Roy?

ROY. Any spare clothes around? Fellows moved off at once. Hit the water with a mighty crack. Hauled myself out - not too bad. Thought I might have pulled a muscle, though. Get these off, then check for bruises. Towel or anything?

SOLVEIG. Think you could lend him your towel, Luse?

ANNA. Of course he can, if he wants. It's under the - no, it's over here.

ROY. Jean's on the way.

Trouble with this kind of bunch. I've given it some thought -

(He removes his coat, shirt and tie)

Good fellows, all of them - but lack a leader. Therefore - thanks, Anna.

ANNA. It's big enough, I hope.

ROY. Therefore - no aim - wander around in little gangs - small bunches of this type. See a solitary fellow - self in this instance. Do him a mischief.

(He ties the towel round his waist and removes

trousers and pants. SOLVEIG and ANNA-LUSE take these garments and hang them to dry on a clothes-horse)

JIRI. What's your answer to this problem, Paul?

SOLVEIG. His name's Roy.

JIRI. Roy.

ROY. It's not clear, really, how far one can get these fellows into a proper group.

(He is now clad only in the towel. He sits down)

Time to time, now, they've been - all of them - offered the chance of one of these -

Sorry. This is yours, Jiri.

JIRI. Why -

ROY. It makes 'group-sense' to have them properly co-ordinated. Take the average group. One of the fellows is put at the head of it. Immediately takes command: should come naturally to him - assuming his character's all-clear, of course. Takes his job: serves his group. Then, though one shouldn't generalise, naturally, there comes a crisis. Fellow in charge - one, makes the plan - two, gives the orders - orders carried out: crisis is weathered.

SOLVEIG. Would you like a hot drink, Roy?

ROY. Then, of course, the lads are better equipped, stronger in consequence: usually far stronger.

JIRI. I've been reading an -

ROY. What sort of drink?

SOLVEIG. Ordinary coffee.

ROY. Just the thing: yes, please. Sorry. Missed that.

20

Again?

JIRI. Reading an article, here, Paul, on the question -

ROY. Roy. Sorry.

JIRI. Roy - an article on, I believe, very much this topic, in fact.

ROY. Conclusions similar to mine, were they?

JIRI. The -

ROY. The conclusions were similar?

JIRI. Conclusions. I'm not sure I - You -

ROY. How did the thing end? The article - What sort of views did they finish by expressing?

JIRI. Views?

ROY. I'm sorry. Haven't been too brusque, have I? You mentioned an article dealing with this problem, wasn't it? Something of this type. My point was - what do they feel about it?

JIRI. What do -

SOLVEIG. Is it all right if we put them to hang sort of like this? Sort of with them hanging outwards so they get the air?

ROY. Moment, Jiri.

(He investigates the garments)

Anything else I can put on while they -

SOLVEIG. Think there's an old dressing-gown somewhere. Luse, can you -

ROY. Anything covering. Just that this isn't too warm. Sorry, Jiri. Something about this article.

ANNA. Last at the back of the cupboard.

JIRI. In fact, Paul, I - these briquettes -

(He rises)

I don't know if you've come across them. I've been
admiring them, you know: very attractive pieces -
possibly worth a high price.

ROY. The - those - ?

JIRI. These ornaments, you know.

ROY. Those little bits of wood?

JIRI. Briquettes.

ROY. What do you find attractive in them?

JIRI. Beg your pardon?

ROY. What do you - what's - what's the point of them?

JIRI. Why, Paul: it is Paul, not -

ROY. Roy. Roy.

SOLVEIG. His name's Roy, Jiri - it's not really all that
difficult to remember.

JIRI. To be candid, Roy, I've taken a fancy - in a small
way, naturally - to some of these briquettes. I'm
proposing to value them - with the aid of these young
ladies, of course.

(SOLVEIG whispers to ROY)

SOLVEIG. Roy... (inaudible)

ROY. What?
Taking - ?

(He frowns. SOLVEIG concludes)

ROY. Well, these briquettes are excellent, Jiri, and of course we'll - we'll evaluate them. Think if we just leave them - leave them where they are for the present. I -

(SOLVEIG has removed a 'briquette' from JIRI's pocket and hands it to ROY, who puts it down on the table, unseen by JIRI)

JIRI. Certainly worth a thought, Paul. I'm glad you're of that opinion. They're fanciful bits of work. Excellent briquettes indeed: the phrase describes them very well.

ROY. Thank you.

(SOLVEIG helps him on with a dressing-gown)

ANNA. Fits all right, does it?

ROY. Pretty reasonable.

(He looks at himself in a mirror. He removes the towel, ties the dressing-gown belt and returns to the group)

New kit.

Wonder if Jean's within call.

(He goes to the door)

Jean.
Jean.

(JEAN appears at the other door)

JEAN. Glad you're still intact after your ducking. Yes - suits you quite well: not bad.

JIRI. Why, Jean: delighted.

JEAN. Jiri: hello. What's that? A magazine.

JIRI. Been admiring, you know, the decor of your room.

JEAN. Have you? Not really my room, though, of course. Have you all been here long?

ANNA. Hello, Jean.

ROY. No: just considering steps we should take, in fact.

(JEAN sits on the table)

JEAN. I don't know, really, if you can do much with this group. Those two are both blind, aren't they?

ROY. We're trying. No problem that can't be met. What I was hoping was to get them into reasonable order - offer them a measure of discipline. Then, if the authorities approve, section may be allowed to continue.

JEAN. Doubtful, really. The strictness is fantastic. Do you think you can control them? I mean, how much discipline can you give them?

ROY. Full treatment, I hoped. Series of exercises: frequent practice. No reason why they shouldn't in the end achieve as much as sighted people. Or better. I've seen blind people work before now, - model of efficiency.

JEAN. But this is just two girls, though. You can give them exercises, but as for turning them into a group -

ROY. What is it exactly happens if they're not up to the standard of efficiency?

SOLVEIG. We've found these for you in the cloakroom: they should be about your size, I think.

JEAN. Nice colour, too.

ROY. Can't say I've ever worn purple trousers before.

SOLVEIG. Do you need any help in putting them on?

ROY. That's - no, no, that's all right. I'll just step -

(He retires behind the screen)

SOLVEIG. Jean. What exercises are you going to recommend?

JEAN. Me? I've got nothing to do with it. Roy's the person to decide.

SOLVEIG. Do you think we could do the exercises?

JEAN. If you tried - most exercises. That is, of course, there are some eye-exercises you couldn't do.

SOLVEIG. And that might impair our efficiency.

JEAN. Only for those exercises. You could do others, of course. I mean -

(ROY appears with the new trousers)

ROY. Fit all right. Only one pocket though. Seem to have forgotten the one on that side.

(He investigates)

JEAN. I was going to ask you, Roy - : that curious incident on the causeway. How did you come to meet the youths?

ROY. No sign of one. Sorry... Youths. How did I meet? Walking along the causeway, I met them. Were about six or seven of them. They addressed a remark to me. I answered: better not to ignore a number, really. Somehow - this was an odd business - they took offence. I tried to smooth things over - no good - pushed me into the - the - the water. Hit it with a crack.

JEAN. And they went off, then?

ROY. Disappeared - cut out quite smartly. Obviously

now, there must be an answer to this sort of thing.
I've given it a good deal of thought, both before and
after the event.

JEAN. Perhaps training them?

ROY. I admit there are no perfect solutions. My aim
would be - co-ordinate them. Trouble is - this kind
of group - as they stand - good fellows, but lack a
leader and wander around in little gangs. If they see
a solitary fellow - naturally they're tempted to do him
a mischief. Who wouldn't be? My answer is - pick
one of the fellows - put him at the head of the group:
immediately takes command - should come naturally
to him. Assuming his character's all-clear, of
course.

JEAN. You're too confident in them. Some of them are
real idiots - very, very little sense of responsibility -
sense of anything.

ROY. Solutions aren't perfect, I agree. I admit. But the
question is, firstly, one of leadership. Fellow takes
his job, serves his group. Then - though one
shouldn't generalise of course, there comes a crisis.
Fellow in charge - one, makes the plan, two, gives
the orders. Orders carried out: crisis is weathered.
The result makes 'group-sense'.

ANNA. Here's a belt.

JEAN. What do you mean by 'group-sense'?

ANNA. Colour's all right with the trousers, is it?

ROY. Blends very well, thank you, Anna. Think I'll just
go and relieve myself, actually, if you can look after
them.

(He goes. JEAN perches on the edge of the table.
Some time elapses. ROY returns)

Group-sense - is the idea. The scheme appeals, too.

ANNA. Anna-Luse.

JEAN. What sort of exercises are you going to give them?
Look, there's just one thing I'd suggest. Give them
short improvisations. Might help in extending their
imagination.

ANNA. Is.

ROY. Give them what?

ANNA. A.

JEAN. You know, short scenes: you put them in a position,
and they have to act as though they were in it.

ANNA. Girl.

ROY. Right. Yes. We'll do that. How was it you said,
exactly?

JEAN. You get them, you put them in a situation - say,
going to the tailor or something, and they have to
behave as though they were in that situation.

ANNA. Cleanliness is essential.

ROY. Going to the tailor?

ANNA. Men.

JEAN. That, or something similar. You see, you want
them to behave in a way outside their normal
experience, make an imaginative leap.

ANNA. Breasts.

ROY. How is this to benefit them? You say they go to the
tailor.

ANNA. Orgasm.

JEAN. Tailor or something similar - something that
allows them to behave differently.

27

ROY. I'll try it. Sounds a - it's a bit out of my reach, frankly - go to the tailor.

JEAN. Needn't be the tailor.

ANNA. Sexuality.

ROY. If you think: we'll try. Perhaps you'll be present, in case the thing takes a wrong turn. Wouldn't want to lose their confidence, you see. Anna.

ANNA. Hello.

ROY. We're trying a - there's a device of Jean's that you may find effective. To do with going to the tailor.

ANNA. Going to the tailor?

ROY. Solveig.

SOLVEIG. Hello, Roy.

ROY. Would you mind coming over here.
Now. I.
Perhaps, Jean - you can explain to them.
Not sure I've -

JEAN. You have to imagine something. Let's say you're at the tailor's. You've asked for a coat. Now you - to be made - Now you come, and you try it on. Let's say it doesn't fit very well and there are a few things wrong with it.

SOLVEIG. We have to take the parts.

JEAN. Yes, each a part.

You can be the tailor, if you like, Solveig, and Anna-Luse - that's right, isn't it? -

ANNA. Anna-Luse.

JEAN. Anna-Luse the customer.

ANNA. I'm the one who's ordered -

JEAN. Sorry, can you speak a bit louder?

ANNA. I'm the one who's ordered the coat.

JEAN. Yes. You come to the office. All right...

SOLVEIG. Shall we begin?

JEAN. When you're ready.

SOLVEIG. How do you like your coat?

ANNA. It's very nice.

JEAN. Can you speak up a bit, Anna?

ANNA. It's very nice.

SOLVEIG. You like it, do you?

ANNA. Yes.

JEAN. Yes, that - That's fine, don't you think, Roy? But
you see - I mean -. I think it would be better if you
didn't like the coat, didn't like the way he has made
it - you object, an argument, etc.

ANNA. I don't like the coat?

JEAN. Yes, you don't, and you say so. All right. When
you're ready.

(Some moments elapse)

ANNA. I don't like the coat.

SOLVEIG. What's wrong with it?

(Some moments elapse)

JEAN. Say something: the point is to get it moving.

29

SOLVEIG. Why don't you like the coat?

ANNA. It's too big, and there's a brood of doves in one of the pockets.

SOLVEIG. Doves? There couldn't be.

ANNA. They are. They're flying all over the pocket.

SOLVEIG. Where?

ANNA. Here.

SOLVEIG. So there are. It must have been one of the broods of doves in the office, they flew into the coat while I was making it, and they've made their home in it.

ANNA. They're mating!

JEAN. Try and make it more realistic.

ANNA. They're mating. They're having sex all over the pocket.

JEAN. No, no, that won't do.

SOLVEIG. Mating? Impossible.

ANNA. They're having orgasms in the pockets.

JEAN. Can you try a more normal approach? If we can't believe it your performance loses interest, you see.

ANNA. Try putting on the coat.

JEAN. What?

ANNA. Put on the coat.

JEAN. No, I'm not in the improvisation.

ANNA. You're in the office. Here's the coat. Quick - a tribe of midgets is clambering out: they've seized you.

SOLVEIG. Really, sir - it's my best product. It's in the most fashionable colour, and you've only mentioned what you thought was wrong. In fact all these things are attractions.

ANNA. It's got too much animal life in it for me to wear it.

JEAN. No, no, you're -

SOLVEIG. My son made it. He can tell the difference between very similar colours.

JEAN. No, no.

ANNA. The colours are very nice to the eye. But the shape: it's almost impossible to get into. Doves, midgets, why, I can see fireworks going off in it.

JIRI. Fireworks?

ROY. What exactly is it you hope to achieve by the exercise? I mean - not running it down, of course.

ANNA. I think people should be told your product is dangerous.

JEAN. It's really a question of exteriorisation - they exteriorise their feelings.

ANNA. Why, the animals are on the rampage - sex every-where.

JEAN. There are positive aspects, though.

SOLVEIG. If you don't like the coat, return it. There are several other customers who -

ANNA. I don't like the coat. I'm going to fight you.

ROY. No.

(He separates the girls)

ROY. They're not to fight - surely. I think -

(He clears his throat)

No. It's over. It's over.

ANNA. Was that all right?

(INGA-LILL enters)

INGA. I've come. Can I help? Hello. Hello, Roy. Hello, Luse.

JEAN. This is Inga-Lill. She was going to assist you with the exercises.

(INGA-LILL embraces ANNA-LUSE)

INGA. Hello, Solveig.

SOLVEIG. Hello.

(They embrace)

INGA. I'll help.

ROY. Have I seen you before?

INGA. No - no, you didn't, but I saw you through a window. There's Jiri - hello.

(She runs over to him)

JIRI. Why - delighted.

INGA. Sorry I disturbed your magazine-reading. Are you watching?

JIRI. I'm - uh. Pardon?

JEAN. Is she all right for the exercises? I thought she'd be able to help in demonstrations.

ROY. I'm glad to have her. She'll have to - She'll have to

32

change, of course - wear jeans, or something, because,
you know -

INGA. Must I? I'm wearing tights now.

ROY. Yes, but for -

JEAN. She's got some jeans. She can easily wear them
if you'd prefer.

ROY. On the whole: yes, if you could.

INGA. Jeans.

JEAN. I'll help you find them.

INGA. If you like.
Sorry, Jiri, see you later. We'll see you in a minute,
Sol and Luse.

(JEAN and INGA-LILL leave)

JIRI. Sorry she had to leave so promptly. Be returning,
will they?

ROY. Must say, I found that scene rather hard to fathom.
I suppose Jean had some purpose behind it.

SOLVEIG. She mentioned exteriorising our feelings.

ROY. Very difficult point. I suppose you think they should
be exteriorised?

SOLVEIG. I don't know. I'm not sure we even exteriorised
them, did we? Did we, Luse?

ANNA. What do you mean by exteriorise?

SOLVEIG. Put out - or outside.

ANNA. Oh. Put out our feelings.

SOLVEIG. Outside feelings.

ROY. Could you find a purpose behind that? I mean - as for me, - I enjoy a scene like that, I suppose, but I ask myself what good does it do. Is it an exercise? Is it for character? Does it have an aim?

SOLVEIG. Both, really.

ROY. I mean, I don't want to be gauche - I'm not suggesting everything whould have a purpose. I enjoyed that scene as much as you did probably..

ANNA. Was I really supposed to dislike the coat?

ROY. Just a minute. Jean seems to have disappeared.

(He goes to the door)

Jean!
Jean!

(INGA-LILL appears at the other door in jeans and blouse)

Ah.

INGA. I hope this is more suitable for your exercises. I left my tunic in the cloakroom.

ROY. It's very good.

INGA. Hello, Jiri. I'm sorry I was away for so long.

(The following conversations occur simultaneously)

INGA. Do you think my new outfit's good? It's for Roy.	ANNA. Can you tell me about Sven while they're discussing this?
JIRI. The - ? For Roy? INGA. For the exercises, you know.	SOLVEIG. Sven? I've told you everything I know, surely.
	ANNA. More. I'm sure there are more details.

ROY. I'd like to do some exercises with them, Jiri, to the end that they become a more viable team. At present this sort of viability makes what I think of as 'group-sense'.

JIRI. Glad to hear it spoken of.

INGA. I'm going to demonstrate and, you see, even if they're blind, they can feel the way I do it. It's simpler than explaining.

JIRI. Simpler? I dare say. What are these exercises?

INGA. I don't know. You know, Roy.

ROY. Viability ones - all-purpose, really. Not sure actually I have the booklet on me - in these trousers - No, rather think they fell into the water when I was attacked by the youths.

JIRI. Attacked? Sounds most hazardous. When did this occur?

INGA. Yes, I saw it from a window. He was pushed in. He wasn't bad though. He shouted at them, struggled out, but

SOLVEIG. Well -

ANNA. What happened on the actual night?

SOLVEIG. It wasn't night: it was late afternoon.

ANNA. Well, then. Yes?

SOLVEIG. We were both rather tired - he'd been playing all day and we went up to his room for a siesta. We slept for about an hour, sort of - you know, sort of holding hands.

ANNA. Yes. Yes.

SOLVEIG. Then we woke up.

ANNA. And -

SOLVEIG. Well, I suppose we - well, I can't really tell you anything that -

ANNA. Tell me.

SOLVEIG. There isn't anything to tell.

ANNA. What was it like?

SOLVEIG. What was what like?

ANNA. Was it easy?

SOLVEIG. Well - I suppose - well, it depends what you mean by easy.

ANNA. Did it hurt?

they had disappeared.

JIRI. Quite a reverse. Did you manage to get some clean clothes?

ROY. Yes, these, in fact.

JIRI. Quick work.

INGA. I like them better than your others.

ROY. Don't feel too happy in purple, really.

JIRI. Why - one of the best - I'd have thought these garments suited you. Most stylish cut.

SOLVEIG. I can't remember now.

ANNA. But surely you remember if it hurt. It always hurts.

SOLVEIG. Yes. I think it did hurt.

ANNA. Yes. Did it? Did you get any - ?

SOLVEIG. What?

ANNA. Was it all right? What did he say?

SOLVEIG. What do you mean?

ANNA. What sort of things did he say, you know, while -

SOLVEIG. Well, I can't -

ANNA. Tell me, you don't tell me anything.

SOLVEIG. It was just - he just - I can't tell you because there isn't anything to tell. It was all perfectly normal. Really, Luse, if you're so curious you only have to try yourself. Some of the -

ROY. Sorry - Solveig. I wonder if you could - Anna. Jean seems to have gone off. Think we should try some of these exercises.

SOLVEIG. Which ones, Roy?

ROY. First get the furniture in order. Clear some space. That -

(He surveys the room from various angles)

These are for viability. They're mobile exercises:
involve movement - that type of thing.
Feeling flexed?

INGA. Is the furniture all right like that?

ANNA. Where should I stand?

ROY. I think - perhaps that chair -

(He adjusts its position)

No.
Can you - in a line - can you stand in a line? In a
line. In a line. Straight line.
Right. These are for mobility.
I want the one in which - Inga - you'll demonstrate,
could you - the one in which you stand on your head,
and move the feet sort of - not exactly on the head -

INGA. Shall I do it?

(She performs the exercise)

ROY. You others - try and get the idea, you know. You
see? Sort of movement with the feet. Sort of foot-
movement. You both watch, I mean - sort of - can
you feel - the -

(SOLVEIG and ANNA-LUSE 'feel' INGA-LILL's
demonstration)

SOLVEIG. I think I've got it.

(She returns to her place and performs the exercise)

ROY. Yes. One. Two.

Keep in time. Not so fast.

(He shouts in SOLVEIG's ear)

ROY. Not so fast.

SOLVEIG. Thanks.

ROY. Right. Now you other two stop. Inga will do it alone.

INGA. Same as before?

ROY. Same exercise.

(INGA-LILL performs the exercise)

I'll hold your feet now.

INGA. Pushing me over -

ROY. Steady.

INGA. It's much easier if you don't -

ROY. Keep the pace.
Right. Next exercise.
On your feet.

SOLVEIG. Which one's this?

JIRI. Paul. I enjoyed that. Something in these exercises.

ROY. Did you, Jiri? Good. That's good.
This next one's good training too.

JIRI. May I have a part?

ROY. I - well - You -
Really the thing to watch, you know - safer, of course.

JIRI. You'd prefer I didn't join you?

(Some moments elapse)

Perhaps I might take a place?

SOLVEIG. Are you joining us, Jiri?

JIRI. Why - Solveig: it is Solveig? Wasn't aware you were
with us. Are you enjoying these exercises?

SOLVEIG. I quite like them. I think I was told they were
good for the figure.

ANNA. They improve breasts.

ROY. All right.
Exercise two. In sections. One -

SOLVEIG. You haven't told us what it is, Roy.

ROY. It's a foot -raising exercise. Raise it in that
direction - right - left foot out - up - out to the side -
arm -

SOLVEIG. Sorry, can Lill demonstrate?

INGA. Not sure I know it very well.

JIRI. I raise my foot, do I?

ROY. It's more a question of -

(He clears his throat)

INGA. As far as I know, I think he means this: is this
right, Roy?

ROY. Along those lines.
Right foot more to the - sorry, left - other foot.

INGA. I touch my left foot with my other hand, though.

ROY. No.

INGA. With the same hand?

ROY. Just a minute.

JIRI. Now, Paul, let's get this straight. Which foot to
which hand? Left or right?

INGA. Jiri, his name's not Paul. There isn't a Paul in the room.

JIRI. Must be confusing him with - his name's not Paul, you say?

ROY. Can you do it? Show the others?

INGA. His name's Roy. It rhymes with boy. Remember that when you want to say it.

JIRI. Now - which foot?

ROY. No, no. It's not a question of - Sorry. Sorry. Can you look at Inga?

JIRI. This young lady?

INGA. Here you are, Sol - you put your left hand...

(She shows SOLVEIG and ANNA-LUSE the position)

ROY. All right? Getting it? Right. One. Two. Keep the pace right. One. Two. Don't drag behind. Anna. Don't drag behind the others.

(He shouts into her ear)

One. Two.

ANNA. Ow.

INGA. Don't shout at her.

ROY. One. Two. Don't fall - don't fall behind.

SOLVEIG. It doesn't help if you shout, Roy. We can hear it quite well if you say it quietly - and not into our ears.

JIRI. Believe I actually feel this exercise doing me good.

ROY. Right. That's it.

JIRI. Very rewarding, Paul. I liked the way you got them
all to do it.

ROY. You did, did you, Jiri? Not always so easy, of course.
Girls with a handicap.

SOLVEIG. They say that blind people can hear better than
others.

ANNA. I know they can.

ROY. Fancy a refreshment?

JIRI. A - ? Perhaps not, Paul, thank you. But I liked that:
found your approach stimulating.

ROY. Here. Your magazine.

JIRI. Mine, is it?

ROY. Now. Something else. Think I'll relieve myself,
first. Inga, can you take charge while I'm gone. Put
them through an exercise or two.

(He goes)

INGA. All right. Break for everybody till he comes back.

(Some time elapses, without much movement.
Roy returns.
Some time elapses)

ROY. We'll -

(Some time elapses)

Right. Any other exercises?

JIRI. Can I apply myself?

ROY. Wouldn't you - don't you think you might prefer to
read your article? I gather it's a very good one. I -

JIRI. To tell you the truth, Paul - Roy. Feel my knee -

the muscles of my knee - freer already - as if transformed. I believe in these exercises.

ROY. I'm glad you do.

I -

Anyone any exercises? Inga?

INGA. No, I -

ROY. Out of ideas.

(He flicks the table)

SOLVEIG. There was a book, somewhere here, which I think had exercises.

ROY. Where?

SOLVEIG. I don't know. I think it's lost.

ROY. Any ideas, Anna?

ANNA. What of?

ROY. Book of exercises.

ANNA. I don't think there's one here. I don't know.

SOLVEIG. I've got an itch in the middle of my back. Can you do something?

ANNA. There?

SOLVEIG. Higher.

ANNA. There?

SOLVEIG. That's it. Ah. That's lovely. Thanks.

ANNA. All right?

SOLVEIG. Mm.

INGA. Is there one there?

ROY. Something.

(He has his hand in a low cupboard)

Kind of black thing - black biscuit.

INGA. Where?

JIRI. May I see? A briquette.

ROY. No, nothing to interest you, Jiri. It's an old - some old pieces of biscuit.

Think if I can just - yes.

(He pulls something out)

INGA. A book. Does it have exercises?

(ROY flips through the book)

ROY. Do the trick, I think. One or two.

INGA. Can I see? It's in a foreign language.

ROY. All right. Now, then. Inga better demonstrate. I'll try and describe this one. Stand in a line.

(He takes a few paces backwards, scrutinising the book)

Right. This one is - touch the -

(He scrutinises the diagram)

No - on the floor. Lying on the floor. Like this.

Look. Inga.

Your feet, feet, feet - like - feet out - knees, yes. Can you copy that, you others?

Now. Back up - back raise. Raise. Bend knees.
Tilt the -

INGA. Can I see it?

(She gets up and looks at the diagram)

Odd exercise. Think I've got it.
All right, Luse and Sol.

(She demonstrates the action)

And you raise your back, and make a sort of little
arch with it. All right?

SOLVEIG. Is that all it is?

INGA. It's very easy. I can't think what the point of it is.

(JIRI has risen)

JIRI. Why, Anna.

ANNA. Hello, Jiri. Do you like the exercise?

JIRI. Remarkable. Her face, you know, Paul, reminds
me of my daughter, my young daughter.

SOLVEIG. Are we supposed to press with our arms? Is
that the point of it?

JIRI. She died, you know. Circumstances of great
difficulty. Very painful.

ROY. Just perform it. Don't worry about the purpose.

JIRI. I myself, unfortunately, I wasn't privileged to be
there.
Paul.

ROY. Yes, Jiri. I'm sorry: I'm trying to -

JIRI. Very similar, have you noticed - your dark-haired
pupil?

ROY. You like her, do you?

ANNA. Me?

JIRI. Very similar, you know, to my young daughter. She
too was -

ANNA. Is it me they're talking about?

ROY. Don't think I met this daughter, Jiri. Could I have?

JIRI. Could you have met her? Why - . No, I fancy you
couldn't.

SOLVEIG. Can we finish the exercise, please, Roy? My
back's getting stiff.

ROY. Right. Up. Relax. Sorry, Jiri. Don't think I ever
met your daughter.

JIRI. Struck me as being, you know, very similar to this
girl. Face, particularly.

ROY. Yes. Right, now. Next exercise.
Lying. Lying down. That's the preliminary position.

(The girls lie on the floor)

Try and keep a space.
Right - feet raised. Raise together. Keep feet together
then. Raise vertical. Think that's right.

(He consults the book)

That's the first part. Wait a bit.

(He fumbles)

Just a moment now. Next bit not too -

(He peruses the book, holds it upside down)

Knees bend, I think. Keep legs as they are, bend the
knees. Keep the legs apart - few inches apart.

JIRI. Paul. That dark-haired girl of yours. Blye eyes. I
wonder if you have noticed. Most similar to my
daughter.

ROY. Is she, Jiri?

JIRI. Most similar. Facial expression, particularly.

ROY. Yes, now you mention it -

JIRI. You agree.

ROY. Might be a resemblance. Yes. Yes. See what you
mean.

JIRI. Do you think it's the hair, or chin, or some other
part?

SOLVEIG. How long do we have to hold this, Roy? My
legs are giving out.

ROY. Just a minute. Could you sit down, Jiri?

(He sits JIRI in a chair and gives him a magazine)

JIRI. Thank you.

ROY. Now you're meant to kick with - with your legs,
somehow. Think that's the -

SOLVEIG. I'm collapsing.

(She lowers her legs)

I just can't. Sorry, Roy. It's a terribly difficult
position.

ROY. All right, others down. On your feet.

SOLVEIG. What was the point of the exercise?

ROY. General mobility.

SOLVEIG. Does it say in the book if it has any special

function?

INGA. Can I see it? You don't mind, Roy?

(She takes the book)

JIRI. Paul. This may interest you. Just come across a passage dealing with very much your line of country.

ROY. I'm pleased you've found something of interest, Jiri.

JIRI. Perhaps you'll permit me to read a little - on the subject of -

SOLVEIG. My knees are sore after that.

ANNA. Mine too.

JIRI. Article is entitled 'One and Many' - and deals with these very problems you were adumbrating. I quote. The difficulty with many of these gangs of wandering troublemakers is their evident lack of a leader. If, thus indisciplined, they meet a solitary person they are liable to do him a mischief. Now, though there can be no final solutions to the problem, the answer may lie in a type of co-ordination. Thus, if one of the troublemakers can be placed at the head of the group, the others will respond: the fellow himself will take command: it should come naturally to him. This assumes that his character is 'all-clear', of course. After a while there comes a crisis. Then the man in charge - one, formulates his plan - two, gives the orders. The orders are carried out - the crisis is weathered. Thus the question is basically one of leadership. The fellow takes his job and serves his group. After a while a spirit of 'group-sense' emerges.

(During the last few lines ROY has been speaking quietly to INGA-LILL. Now she approaches JIRI)

INGA. Hello, Jiri. Shall we sit down a moment?

JIRI. What sort of comment would you make?

(INGA-LILL helps him to sit down)

INGA. I wonder if you're at all hungry. Or tired. I could show you a room.

JIRI. No; it's a kind offer, but I fancy I'm well-placed at this instant. Interested by some of the work of your young leader. Find the way he wears his authority quite stimulating.

INGA. Yes. He is good, isn't he?

ROY. Another exercise.

INGA. Now.

(She puts an arm round JIRI)

I'm sure we get on very well together. Do you like my hair?

ROY. This one on the floor again. Stomachs. Lying on stomachs.

SOLVEIG. The floor's cold. Can't we have a standing-up one?

INGA. You can feel it if you like. It's quite fine. It's said to go well with my eyes. Red hair, you see: green eyes.

ROY. Have to go by the book. Down there in black and white, you see.   .

INGA. You like it? Perhaps you'd like to come outside. I know somewhere quiet where we can go and be alone and -

JIRI. Why - Fancy I've noticed a -

(He rises and walks across the room)

JIRI. Another briquette. Paul!

ROY. Yes.

JIRI. I wonder. How much is this going for? Fair price,
     I'd imagine. Reflects the light.

INGA. Oh, Jiri. Please don't. That's my hairgrip. It's
     not a briquette. Please don't go wild.

JIRI. I beg your - A hairgrip?

ROY. Jiri, would you - Inga, here, would like to take you
     for a walk. She's got a collection of briquettes: they're
     all very nice. She'll show you them.

JIRI. A collection? Why, very much so, How do we get
     there?

INGA. I'll take you. It's out this way. Give me your arm.
     There.

JIRI. I'm attracted, Paul, I must confess, by the thought
     of these objects. I trust my leaving won't inconvenience
     you.

ROY. That's all right, Jiri.

JIRI. Where were these briquettes?

     (He leaves with INGA-LILL. ROY mops his brow with
     his handkerchief)

ROY. Now. Right.

SOLVEIG. Can we have a bit of a rest, Roy? I think my
     legs would just collapse if we go on.

ROY. This is a simple one.
     Lying down. Feet -

     (He adjusts the girls' feet)

     Now.

(He looks at the paper)

Not quite it.
Should be on a cushion.
Here.

(He takes two cushions and gives one to each of the
girls)

Under your stomachs. That's it.

(He adjusts the cushions)

Got them? Now.
Seems you have to push. Push with your legs.

SOLVEIG. How? Backwards?

ROY. Just a minute.
No. Wait.

(He scrutinises the book, holds it upside down. A page
falls out, onto the floor)

Damn. Book's falling to pieces.

SOLVEIG. Do we have to crawl about like turtles, you
mean?

ROY. Object is mobility. It's a mobile aim. Group-sense.

(SOLVEIG sits up)

SOLVEIG. It's not a very mobile position. I can't think
what it's for. I'm sure it would make you less mobile.

ROY. Hold on.

(He takes the book to the table, scrutinises the page)

SOLVEIG. What's the book called? Does it have a title?

ROY. Just a minute.
Title page missing.

ANNA. What language is it in? Can you read some of it to us?

(INGA-LILL enters)

INGA. Gave him a sleeping pill.
Jean says these are prenatal exercises.

SOLVEIG. What?

INGA. Prenatal.

SOLVEIG. Ones for expectant mothers? Yes, I thought you didn't have to crawl about like that in ordinary ones.

ROY. You sure of that?

INGA. Jean said they were. I gave Jiri a sleeping pill and left him sitting against one of those large waste-paper bins.

ROY. Took it, did he? Took the pill?

INGA. He was about to take it. I put it in his hand with a glass of water.

ROY. Something bound to distract him before he takes it.

INGA. Hello, Luse.

ANNA. Hello.

ROY. Right. Have to jettison these then. Try another tack.

(JIRI enters)

JIRI. Paul. Why - . Putting these girls through their drill, are you?

(ROY does not reply)

ROY. Can you entertain him, Inga?
Just give my face a wash.

(He goes over and dips his handkerchief in the bowl of water. He sponges his forehead)

ANNA. Hello, Jiri.

JIRI. Why - Anna, I believe. Ha: you know - I may not have told you - you resemble a young daughter of mine.

ROY. Right. Try some co-ordination now.

JIRI. Remarkably similar facial features.

ANNA. Her hair was like mine, was it?

JIRI. Same style, yes. I fancy you're embodied in her. Remarkable.

(He takes a large red handkerchief from his pocket and blows his nose)

Why -

ROY. Think you might sit down, Jiri? When you've finished using that handkerchief, of course.

JIRI. Paul: wonder if I mentioned it to you: this pupil of yours - exactly the same features as my daughter - deceased you know: a trifle prettier, perhaps - eyes a shade bluer?

ROY. Inga.

INGA. Hello, Roy.

ROY. Here a moment.

(INGA-LILL comes over. She stands in front of ROY)

Just a minute.

(He kisses her on the mouth. She responds balletically, standing on one toe)

All right. Jiri.

JIRI. I -

ROY. Could you -

(He mops his brow with his handkerchief)

Over here.

(He takes JIRI over to the sofa)

Now, if you could - sit down -

JIRI. Delighted. Might witness some of your work. Unless,
of course, you preferred me to participate?
Can't properly express how, after the one I performed
with you, how much a feeling of wellbeing suffused me.
Felt myself restored: most harmonious effects.
Believe my daughter, too, was helped by these
exercises.

ROY. Was she?

(He turns away and stands as though he may fall, then
collapses into INGA-LILL's arms.
INGA-LILL strokes his hair. ROY disengages himself)

All right. Co-ordination. Anna, want you to stand
there.

ANNA. Where? Here?

(ROY adjusts her position)

ROY. You're to give orders. Frame an order - deliver it:
pat. Try for it spot-on.

ANNA. What?

(ROY takes a breath)

ROY. You deliver an order. You're in charge of Sol -
Solveig and the other girl, Inga-Lill. Tell them to do
something and they do it.
Oh, God.

(He embraces INGA-LILL)

INGA. Come on. You're all right. You don't have to do
that.

(ROY disengages himself)

ROY. Right. Kick off.

(He sits down)

ANNA. What must I do? I'm sorry.

INGA. You give orders.

ANNA. What sort?

INGA. Any. You tell us to do things and we do them.

JIRI. Paul: must confess, I'm transfixed by her appearance.
Resembles my daughter, you know.
Well-featured, too.

ANNA. Solveig - go over there and pick up that piece of
paper.

SOLVEIG. Certainly.

(She performs this task)

ANNA. Done? Lill -

ROY. Right - no. Solveig takes over.

SOLVEIG. Inga is to take the waste-paper basket and move
it an inch to the right.

INGA. Certainly.

(She performs the action)

JIRI. Why - a brisk idea. Entertaining scheme, Paul.

(ROY, in distraction, impulsively kisses ANNA-LUSE

on the mouth.
He disengages himself. Some moments elapse)

ANNA. Roy?

INGA. Why did you do that?

ANNA. Roy?

ROY. All right. Next. Inga.

ANNA. Roy?

INGA. Why? Why did you - ? What did you do it for?

ROY. Inga. Go ahead. Your order. This is a leadership
exercise, strengthens the -

ANNA. Roy? Can I have Roy again?

JIRI. Why, Paul - I'm struck, struck by this performance.

ANNA. Roy?

(She begins to take quick, shallow breaths)

INGA. You've done it.

SOLVEIG. What's the matter, Luse?

ANNA. Roy.

ROY. Can we get on, now? Energies bent -

SOLVEIG. What's happened?

ANNA. Roy.

(She makes clutching movements with her hands)

ROY. Inga. Your order. Your order.

INGA. Can't you do something about her?

SOLVEIG. What is it, Inga?

INGA. He's been stupid.

ROY. Well, Jiri - that looks a worthwhile article. Dare say you've been reading it.

JIRI. Informative, yes. I was hoping you might try it. Advice they give is good, too.

ROY. What sort of thing do they say?

INGA. Aren't you going to do anything? You can't just leave her.

JIRI. It deals with -

ROY. Go away: it's not important - can't do a thing.

JIRI. I beg your pardon.

INGA. At least look after her. Do something to help.

ROY. What can I do?

JIRI. My opinion the view is well presented.

(ROY looks at ANNA-LUSE, goes over to her and gives her another kiss. ANNA-LUSE groans and sobs)

ROY. There. All's well. Nothing to -

(ANNA-LUSE sobs and pants loudly)

SOLVEIG. Are you all right, Luse?

ROY. Leave her alone. Girl's all right.
Now then.

SOLVEIG. All right?

(She embraces ANNA. ANNA continues to sob)

INGA. You're idiotic. What are you going to do?

56

ROY. Girl's highly strung. She'll calm. Meanwhile set the place for some further work.

ANNA. Hold me.

SOLVEIG. What is it?

ANNA. I want to feel you. I want to feel you. I want to feel your breasts. I want to feel you. Hold me. Roy. Roy.

SOLVEIG. Why do you want Roy?

ROY. Right. Question and answer test. Simple discipline. Solveig. Over here, please.

SOLVEIG. Something's the matter with Luse.

ROY. Leave her. She's just tense. Now. Inga.

SOLVEIG. You'll be all right.

(She goes towards ROY)

ROY. Question and answer. Solveig. That table - on that table there are three objects. Want you to go over, discover what they are - best of your abilities - report back to me.

SOLVEIG. All right.

(She goes to the table)

INGA. Can I do something?

ROY. Wait till she's finished.

(SOLVEIG returns)

Right?

SOLVEIG. One bowl, which contained water. Also soap, flannel, and a book.

ROY. Right. Inga's turn.

INGA. What do I have to do?

JIRI. Am I included in this?

ROY. Just wait, Jiri - your turn's next.

> Inga - now.
> A description of Solveig. Look at her. Take in the
> features. Then describe her.
>
> (INGA surveys SOLVEIG)
>
> Right. Turn away.
>
> Now.

INGA. Blonde hair, fairly straight, shoulder length.
Grey-blue eyes. Regular features. Slim waist. Bust
smallish.

ROY. That will do. All right.

SOLVEIG. You haven't described my character.

ANNA. I'm pregnant.

INGA. I don't have to describe that. Shall I describe her
clothes? They're not her most exciting ones - you
should be in that nice hat - that sort of blue beret -
which she wears with a slight tilt.

ANNA. I've got Roy's baby.

SOLVEIG. Are you all right, Luse?

ANNA. I've got Roy's baby.

ROY. Ignore her. Bit overstrung. Now - Inga again.

JIRI. Fancied that I - I was included, Paul. Won't have
to lose my chance, will I?

ROY. What would you like to do?

JIRI. Tell you the truth, Paul: that briquette, you know. One over there. Wonder if I'd be permitted a closer examination. Wanted to compare it with the lining of my pocket.

ANNA. My periods have stopped: I'm going to have Roy's baby.

ROY. Could you keep her quiet, Inga. Certainly, Jiri: go ahead.

JIRI. I may, may I?
Delighted.

(He goes over)

Attractive object: quite a -

(He examines it)

Need to compare it with others, I fancy.
Yes.

ROY. You like it, do you, Jiri?

JIRI. I was comparing it, you see, with these others. It's a fine jewel: novelty-product, I believe.

ROY. Yes, it's a good novelty: not many of them about at present.

JIRI. I can believe it: why, a novelty of this sort - not frequently met with.

ANNA. I'm going to be sick. Sol -

(She falls to her knees and retches, putting her hand to her mouth)

INGA. What's - Shall I get you something?

(ANNA-LUSE breathes deeply)

SOLVEIG. Are you all right, Luse?

JIRI. I understand that few of these novelties are available. And, to me, they are genuine novelties.

ANNA. I'm having Roy's baby.

INGA. I'll see if I can get Jean.

(She runs out)

JIRI. Genuine products.

SOLVEIG. Come and sit over here.

ROY. Can you leave her, Solveig? Don't need to encourage her.

SOLVEIG. I'm only helping her to sit down.

ANNA. Don't want to.

SOLVEIG. Get up from there, at least. Come on. You can't stay on the floor.

JIRI. Really genuine, are they, Paul?

ANNA. I'm having Roy's baby.

SOLVEIG. Come on: up.

ANNA. Want to lie down.

SOLVEIG. Come on.

ANNA. I'm having the baby. I can feel it. There.

SOLVEIG. Come on, don't be silly.

(ANNA stands in front of the table, breathing heavily)

ANNA. No.

No.

(SOLVEIG kisses her on the cheek)

ANNA. Roy.
   I'm going to be sick. Get me a - I'm going to be sick.
   Roy. Roy. Roy.

SOLVEIG. Sh.

JIRI. Now that - that one may prove to be of inferior make.
   Only one test in these cases. I have others, in my
   pocket - I compare -

ROY. Can you do something about her? Could you get
   Jean? Jean I think's the one.

SOLVEIG. I can't leave Luse like this, though. She's not
   at all well. I think she may be sick.

ROY. Best thing's not to encourage her if she's in this
   state. Question of control, you see.
   Can you get Jean, now. She'll deal with it. Jiri -

JIRI. I -

SOLVEIG. Have to go, Luse. Will you be all right there?
   I'll be back. I'll just be fetching Jean. All right, won't
   be long.

ROY. Now. Move over here perhaps. Take these objects.
   I'd like your advice on a point or two.

   (They move to the sofa)

JIRI. Delighted.

ANNA. Roy. I can't. Roy. No.

ROY. Now: shall we sit down?

ANNA. Help me. I -

   (She takes a deep breath)

   Don't want to -

ROY. Getting rough, isn't it? Sorry about the interruptions. This point needs concentration.

(ANNA-LUSE, who has been resting against the table now begins to crawl onto it, and lies on her back in the 'delivery-position')

It was chiefly about these youngsters - bunch of eight or nine - I encountered this morning. Nothing of course on this occasion. Bit of water never harmed anyone. Next time, however - one never knows - tougher things round the corner perhaps. I'll be frank - I wonder, could you put in a word for me - possibility of being transferred?

JIRI. Of being - ? Not certain I have your meaning. Something to do with - ?

ROY. I'll make it clearer.

(Most of ANNA-LUSE's subsequent speeches consist of incomprehensible and semi-comprehensible phrases - groans, sobs and screams characteristic of the pains of childbirth)

ANNA. Solveig. It's coming. I don't -

(She shrieks)

I don't want it.
Uh - Solv -

(She screams)

Roy.

JIRI. Is the girl in any trouble? Should we assist?

(He rises)

ROY. No, no. No, no. Nothing. Not important.

(He sits JIRI down again)

ROY. Next part demands some attention. Hub of the argument. Question is - are these characters - these youngsters - or any other - likely to attack again?

JIRI. You're referring - to the - this earlier incident?

ANNA. I don't. I don't. Not again. Not - no. No.

JIRI. The occasion you were pushed into the water?

ANNA. It can't do it.

(She sobs, and chokes. A long scream follows)

JIRI. Why - Seems to be in an extremity.

(He rises again)

Peculiar. Is this an exercise?

ROY. Yes. One of the newer ones. It's a lung-stretching exercise - full play of the vocal cords, you see. Sorry you have to be in on it.

JIRI. Why, Paul - can't say I enjoy the sight of her in this extremity. Reminds me of a -

ROY. Would you like to sit down?

JIRI. I may have noted earlier - I find her peculiarly similar to a young daughter of mine, now deceased.

(ANNA-LUSE sobs)

Name was Livia.

ROY. Similar to this one, was she? Shall we sit down?

(He helps JIRI to sit)

JIRI. Similar? She was: strikingly so.
Shade of hair, you know, especially.

ROY. How was it she died?

ANNA. It's coming. I can't. I can't. No. I can't.

(She gasps)

JIRI. I beg your pardon.

ROY. Your daughter.

ANNA. Rbgv. Rd. Rgr.

(The sounds rise to a protracted scream)

JIRI. Becoming difficult to hear you, Paul.

(ANNA-LUSE sobs)

ROY. Just wondering how your daughter -

JIRI. That? Well now. Some time since it happened. It was shortly after she was married. Husband was -

(The rest of the sentence is drowned by ANNA-LUSE's cries. JIRI rises.
ROY rises and goes over to ANNA-LUSE)

ROY. Keep your voice lower.

ANNA. Roy.

(She gasps. INGA-LILL enters)

INGA. No sign of Jean.

ANNA. I can't. It's not. I don't want to.

INGA. What's happened?

ROY. Girl's got a stomach-pain. Thought it best to leave her. Like to come over and join us? We're discussing the question of control.

INGA. What did you do to her?

ROY. Jiri and I have been having -

INGA. What did you do to her?

ANNA. Roy.

ROY. No need to raise your -

INGA. What did you - ? What did you do? What did you do?
Let me - leave me alone.

ROY. Voice down - best not to encourage her. Come over
and sit -

INGA. Leave me.

(They struggle)

Leave me. Let me.

(She shouts and bites ROY's jacket)

ROY. Hold on.

ANNA. Roy.

INGA. What did you do to her, you idiot?

(ROY is holding her against the wall. She presses
forward and kisses him on the mouth, then disengages
herself rapidly and strikes him on the face with her
fist. ROY stumbles, a hand to his eyes.
INGA-LILL goes over to ANNA-LUSE)

Are you all right? What is it?

ANNA. I'm having Roy's baby. I can't. Do something. No.
No.

(She screams and chokes)

INGA. Hold on. I'll get you some -

(She goes over to the bowl of water)

ANNA. Roy.

JIRI. Paul.

(ROY stands, transfixed, between his appellants. He moves towards JIRI)

I was considering. A small company might be formed, and the value of these briquettes preserved.

(ROY sits on the sofa)

What's your view?

Prefer to consider the matter?

(INGA-LILL smooths ANNA-LUSE's forehead with a wet handkerchief. ANNA-LUSE continues to sob)

ANNA. No. No.

INGA. You'll be all right. Is that better?

ANNA. I want. I -

INGA. There. Is that cooler? Sh.

JIRI. You're with my main point, are you? Evidently, in the normal course of things, these objects would be lost, or otherwise displaced.

ANNA. I can't. It's worse. Give me. I can't have it. Inga. I can't.

INGA. (Simultaneously) What did you do to her? What did you do? Why didn't you help her?

ROY. (Also simultaneously) Could you keep - No. Sorry, Jiri. I can't do - nothing else I - can't you find Jean for me?

JIRI. Now, Paul, A small company, you see.

ANNA. I'm going to die. I'm going to die.

INGA. Look what you've done to her. How did you do it?

ANNA. I want to die. I want to die. Inga. Do something.

(She sobs and screams, her voice becoming hoarse)

I don't want to have it -

Uh -

(She begins to 'bear down', groaning rhythmically.
INGA-LILL massages her shoulders)

INGA. It's all right. You're all right. It's all right.

(The groaning becomes feverish and determined)

JIRI. So you see, Paul: a small company could be formed -
this would safeguard these products. It would,
naturally, be distressing if these objects were to be
lost to the -

ROY. Nothing to do with me. She can't - can't you turn
her off the table? Can't continue indefinitely.

INGA. Bite on that. There.

(She puts a folded handkerchief between ANNA-LUSE's
teeth. The breathing becomes ferocious)

ROY. What do you - You can't expect me to watch, Inga.
Can't you get her off the table.

(ANNA-LUSE groans and shouts through the handkerchief)

JIRI. The possibilities are wide, here, and I dare say,
Paul, you might be persuaded to assist.

ROY. We're leaving. I'm going out. Jiri - we're going
out. We'll discuss the - we're - this way.

(He takes JIRI out hurriedly)

INGA. There.

ANNA. Roy.

INGA. Sh.

ANNA. I can't. I can't. I can't. Worse. Inga. I can't have
it. I don't want. It's coming. I can't. Do something.
Do something. Roy's b- -.

(She shouts meaningless words. INGA-LILL shouts)

INGA. You're all right. Hold my -

(ANNA-LUSE seizes INGA's hands and tries to pull her
towards her)

You're all right. Sh.

(Abruptly ANNA-LUSE stops moving)

ANNA. It's better. It's better. It's better. I can't feel it.

(ROY enters)

INGA. You're all right.

ANNA. I can't feel it. It's better. Coming. Coming. I can
feel -

ROY. Can we stop this now? Time we -

(His words are drowned by the culminating scream of
ANNA-LUSE's agony as the 'baby' crowns.
ROY pales.
After another scream ANNA-LUSE falls back)

ANNA. Finished. It's born. I -

(She lies motionless. INGA-LILL holds the 'baby'
in her hands. She severs the umbilical cord)

My baby. My baby.

(INGA-LILL surveys the creature)

ANNA. Is it all right? Is it breathing?

INGA. Yes. It's -

ANNA. Give it - give it to me.

INGA. Washed...

(She washes the 'baby' in the bowl)

ANNA. Give me my baby.

(INGA-LILL dries the 'baby')

ROY. Can we end this now, Inga? Can you get her up?
Anna -

ANNA. Give me my baby.

INGA. What shall I do?

ROY. I'll take the creature.

INGA. No.

ANNA. Roy. Roy.

INGA. He's got the baby.

ANNA. Roy. Give me the baby. Roy. Give me - Roy.

(She lifts her head, stretches out her arms)

ROY. Can you keep her quiet?

INGA. Give her the baby.

ROY. There's no baby.

ANNA. Give me the -

ROY. There's no baby.

ANNA. Give me -

INGA. Don't kill it, Roy.
  Don't -

ANNA. No -

  (She screams)

  Don't kill it. Don't. Don't kill it. Roy.

  (She screams several times. ROY strangles the 'baby')

ROY. There.

INGA. No.

ROY. There.

  (He drops the 'baby' onto the floor.
  He kicks it once, and again. He then retches, stumbles
  across to the window, and vomits out of it.
  ANNA-LUSE is on her knees in front of the table,
  making regular choking sounds.
  INGA-LILL tries to revive her. After a while ROY
  returns from the window. He washes his face in the
  bowl of water. JIRI appears)

JIRI. Paul?
  Why - Paul was here, wasn't he? Paul?

  (ROY looks at him)

  I've been struck, you know, by an idea: may turn out
  to be profitable.

ANNA. What did he do with it?

JIRI. Just this - the setting up of a small company - the
  forming of a small trust, you know.

ROY. Yes.

JIRI. This - yes, you see - would enable either of us to
  purchase these objects, and others, of course, at a
  much lower rate than would normally be -

ANNA. Where is it?

(She begins to stumble round the room, arms extended,
feeling for the child. INGA sits in a daze)

Where is it? Where is it?

JIRI. At a lower rate, you see, Why, Paul, sure you'll
enter this scheme -

ANNA. Baby? Baby?

ROY. Sounds - Yes, I -

JIRI. I know you have an eye for some of these objects.
Such a trust, you see, would enable greatly reduced
expenses to - Why -

ANNA. Baby?

ROY. What exactly would the object be?

JIRI. I beg your pardon?

ROY. What's the - what's the point of the scheme?

JIRI. The point? The purchasing of these briquettes.

ROY. Purchasing of briquettes?

ANNA. He threw it. He threw it out. It out. It's there.
Out of the window.

(Some moments elapse)

It can fly. It can fly. It can fly. It can fly. It can fly.
It's flying. It's flying back to me. It was born with
wings.
It's flying.

JIRI. Flying, is it? The briquettes, you see, are
purchased more cheaply.

(ROY does not respond)

JIRI. Can I count on your support?

Yes?

You will assist, will you? A scheme not to be missed.

You'll help in the venture?

(ROY does not move)

I can have your support, can I?

(ROY does not respond)

Or - discretion. Prefer not to commit, perhaps: this stage.

Perhaps the wisest course.

You - ?

(Some time elapses)

Perhaps later?

(ROY fails to respond.
JIRI, after a while, disappears, raising his eyebrows in perplexity.
ROY walks to the centre of the stage.
Slowly his hands come up to his eyes.
He begins to wail in the manner of a new-born baby, his body assuming a foetus-like position)

ANNA. Roy!

(An expression of wonder comes over her face)

Roy!

(She stumbles over to him, and holds him as though he were a baby. She stares ahead of her. Some moments elapse)

I can see. I can see.

ANNA. Fields, trees, babies, fires, clothes, chocolate, music, water, songs, pleasure, babies, water.

(Her eyes do not move. ROY continues to scream.
ANNA-LUSE begins to sob, crying out and laughing
in a kind of hysterical ecstasy. She makes a gesture
of lifting her breast and, with a transfigured expression
on her face, places her nipple to ROY's mouth)

JENS
1965

JENS was first presented by University of Sussex
Theatre on 14th June 1965. It was directed by the
Author, with the following cast:

BIRGER	Sarah Lawrence
ING-BRITT	Jill Evans
BRAATOY	Bob Lacey
PEART	Grahame Walshe
HORSE	Richard Fox
HEN	Shifrah Fram
LORETTE	Janice Ballantine
SANDIE	Patricia Napier
TEACHER	Charlotte Townsend
JANIE	Barbara Rogers
TIBS	Patrick Nevill
LOUYS	Roger Tucker
GJORDA	Sylvia Picciotto

BRAATOY. Ing-Britt - we'll start this one over -

By this side.

Nearer the - a little - yes.

Now, Sandie. You'll come - you'll - from this - from this side.

SANDIE. From here?

BRAATOY. Now a few paces towards Ing-Britt - then, once you reach her - two paces more in that direction.

Would you like to try that now?

(SANDIE performs the action)

ING-BRITT. I'm meant to look at the wall?

BRAATOY. Yes: that was quite good.

As she approaches you can look towards her. Try that again with more -

With more - Sandie: a look towards her: you see Ing-Britt's face - you move to front.

PEART. Hen's getting restless.

BRAATOY. Would you like to perform that?

PEART. Keep down: watch the action.

BIRGER. I'll take care of it.

SANDIE. All right.

(She performs the action)

PEART. Looked all right from here.

Chicken's being a bit distracting.

BIRGER. I'll preoccupy it. Come on, dearie.

BRAATOY. That's improving.

Did you - any of you others have any comments you'd like to make?

Sandie?

SANDIE. No, I'm happy with it.

PEART. I'd like to see more attention from the animals.

BIRGER. Hen wasn't misattending - it hasn't eaten for some time, though, and it's excited.

BRAATOY. Would the hen like to perform?

ING-BRITT. It's likely to stall: might be all right.

PEART. Needs respect. Come on, Maudie - that its name?

Respect the boss. Want to try the mat?

BIRGER. It can't make up its mind.

It's very sweet really.

Come on, Maudie.

(She whispers)

BRAATOY. More of that seemed satisfactory.

ING-BRITT. Perhaps I should nearer chimney.

BIRGER. Yes - Maud will do it. She'll perform.

PEART. Make sure the creature's clean.

BIRGER. Stand in the centre: yes, she's all right. I checked her.

BRAATOY. Come on, Maudie - that's the right name, is it? I don't want to queer the animal from the start.

HEN. Yes.

PEART. Show respect.

HEN. Yes.

BRAATOY. She's a bit awkward - but we'll have her presently at ease.

Who'll act with her?

BIRGER. I will: I don't mind.

Oh, sorry.

(She comes over)

Maudie: I'm going to act with you.

(The HEN whispers)

PEART. Get the creature to respect Braatoy - other we don't know where we'll be.

BIRGER. She's telling me about her last meal.

BRAATOY. Stand here, Maudie - in front of this chair. Now - don't sit yet. One hand on - one hand on the chair - on the - yes.

Birger comes - Birger comes with a casket - can you get one?

(SANDIE offers a casket)

BIRGER. Thanks, Sandie.

BRAATOY. Present the hen to the casket... is what you have to do, Birger.

PEART. Maudie -

BRAATOY. You kneel, present the thing -

PEART. Keep your eyes up - respect the chief - don't twitch.

BIRGER. As an offering, or -

BRAATOY. Yes, you present it to him.

All right.

BIRGER. Yes: hold on, Maudie.

Don't let...

(She whispers)

BRAATOY. All right now?

BIRGER. Yes.

(She performs the action)

HEN. Am I to take the casket?

BRAATOY. That was nicely done. Thank you, Birger.

HORSE. Was impressive, Birger - effective display - very much enjoyed.

BIRGER. There's some toffee in it.

You're not writing too much down, I hope.

HORSE. Keeping you charted, that's all.

PEART. Let go of the chair. Section's over.

80

Hen's become uncooperative.

(The HEN releases the chair)

Right: take a corner.

LORETTE. A large black crow has stopped an old woman.

Asking it the way.

BRAATOY. Lorrie, we'll have you on the job now.

LORETTE. A large crow... making route-enquiries.

BRAATOY. Couldn't be. Over here. Yes. An interim-system.

Ing-Britt falls - I'll show you the spot.

Ing-Britt.

(He demonstrates)

Hurts an ankle - and you appear - three paces.

HORSE. She's got a tooth to it: offering it a -

PEART. Don't interrupt the boss: you're spoiling the system.

HORSE. Simply observing what's going on in the - might be a matter of some importance. Not distracting Braatoy, am I?

PEART. Get across.

SANDIE. Don't hurt the horse. What he says is probably true.

HORSE. I don't see how he can expect me to - uh -

(He falls over the chair)

PEART. Horse took a tumble.

SANDIE. He's hurt his leg. I told you to -

Poor Matthew.

PEART. Keep the thing quiet.

SANDIE. He needs a mustard-bath.

BRAATOY. This thread - take the red swyre. Threaded
through the chair - you join it. When it's tugged... a
moment of response.

HORSE. I'm all right: thought the fellow had damaged by
books.

SANDIE. What's in them? All these? You can tell me. My
name's Sandie.

BRAATOY. Take the end. First, Ing-Britt - look at the
wall.

ING-BRITT. This?

BRAATOY. Look at that wall, yes.

Lorrie.

LORETTE. Hello.

BRAATOY. The other end: left hand.

SANDIE. The last light's gone.

BRAATOY. Ah, string's out - can't have been strong.

(Some moments elapse. BRAATOY investigates)

HORSE. D'you suppose this has more significance than the
last one? And if so, where would it lie?

BRAATOY. Take that end.

SANDIE. Hard to say: watch Lorrie closely.

HORSE. She's one of the newer ones, isn't she?

SANDIE. Lorrie? No, about the same.

How's your foot?

HORSE. Not in bad condition: it was more that roughster that worried me. Didn't seem to know a limit.

SANDIE. Try walking.

(The TEACHER enters)

TEACHER. Ah, Braatoy: may I have a few words?

I'd like to consult.

I'd like to see Braatoy, if I may.

PEART. Wait till he's finished.

TEACHER. Ah, now.

(She coughs)

Braatoy, I have - ah - a little news about developments.

BRAATOY. I'm pleased to hear them.

We were just measuring the base of this chair.

TEACHER. Now: it is - is it - all right for these others to hear the - these news.

Ah, Ing-Britt: hello, dearie.

ING-BRITT. Hello...

BRAATOY. I don't think there's any - they should have your report.

SANDIE. This is one of the teachers.

TEACHER. Ah: yes: I like your group.

Actually, there have been some problems - none
insoluble, but - some moments of difficulty.

Miss Petersen was locked in the shed.

PEART. Locked?

BRAATOY. Alone, or - ?

TEACHER. There were - no: the children were there too,
they're having a competition of some sort, involving -

PEART. Want to sit down?

TEACHER. Thank you.

(She sits)

Torture has been offered.

BRAATOY. On Miss Petersen?

TEACHER. They've all split up into groups, you know.
The torture's offered competitively.

(She accepts a bun from PEART)

Thank you.

HORSE. Interested in this development, I must say. Have
a feeling it might lead into something of note.

BRAATOY. Mental torture, was this?

TEACHER. Yes, that -

That figured too, I believe.

Oh, I've crumbed your carpet.

BRAATOY. That's all right.

PEART. Was one little lad, Colin, involved in this?

84

TEACHER. Colin - yes - ah - one of the leader-groups.

HORSE. Would you say this had any larger significance?

TEACHER. Goodness, I -

BIRGER. You needn't answer the horse - he's -

He's got a number of questions. Doesn't seem to know when to stop.

HORSE. I'm rather disappointed by that, Birger.

TEACHER. I'm not altogether sure how well Miss Petersen is taking this.

HORSE. You'd rather she witheld these questions, would you?

TEACHER. Their - the children's idea of pain, you see -

Don't seem, really, to be aware of its possibilities.

HORSE. Frankly disturbed by that, Birger.

TEACHER. It has immense possibilities. They try to extract - with each fresh bout - a different sort of cry from her: and to a large extent succeed.

BIRGER. Try and sit down - you'll disturb the chief, soon.

TEACHER. Some of them don't make her suffer at all -

One simply the sniffing of various large, dark flowers.

But others, you know, others - she finds difficult to bear.

SANDIE. Shall I let the horse take this measurement?

BIRGER. He switches his interests easily - come on, Matthew.

HORSE. Birger - I've felt for some little time that you were sympathetic to some of these questions. Now's the time to try you.

BIRGER. I didn't mean that.

BRAATOY. What about other, more general, developments?

The recent meeting. The children's diet -

TEACHER. Thank you.

(She accepts an orange from BRAATOY)

The meeting -

The blind - you know the blind young fellow - freckles - plays a flute, I believe -

D'you have a knife for this?

PEART. I'll - yes - just - .

TEACHER. A knife. Yes, I -

This fellow was put into a competition - won it - probably through default.

They gave him a cello.

HORSE. Yes, I - I was glad to hear you say that. I was present at the meeting, actually, and notified - noted the - this - , and -

Actually I was puzzled by the gift of a cello. Can he play?

TEACHER. I don't know if he's musical. Most of the children, of course, are taught rudiments. And one comes across adults who listen - hiding themselves away, try and capture hints taught to the children.

HORSE. No, he couldn't play. This what stranged the

encounter.

PEART. Blunt one.

HORSE. He was given the cellist - the cello.

TEACHER. I never heard what he did with it. Didn't -
didn't seem to know what it was for.

PEART. I'll try that. Give me the cutter.

TEACHER. He understood the meaning of the gift.

HORSE. But that's not enough for most of us to understand
what he meant. Let me try to explain: if I write an
account, I have to clarify the scene - I take events -
you and I do...

But events by themselves are events.

BRAATOY. Could you distract him a little, Birger, with
some object?

HORSE. They're not events.

BRAATOY. A toy, maybe, or food.

HORSE. I'll try and be plain - here are the events.

What's this? No, I won't take this just now.

TEACHER. I don't see the horse is wrong - but his angle
is unfamiliar.

HORSE. I'll demonstrate. Can you put this aside?

BIRGER. Come on, I'll introduce you to Ing-Britt.

HORSE. Can I just demonstrate this point - I'll use these
objects.

Objects are events: then there's the image of them.
An image itself must relate them.

ING-BRITT. Come over here.

(She takes him further back.

Stands looking at him for some time)

TEACHER. A very pleasant orange, Peart.

PEART. Found it in the cupboard.

TEACHER. The children are given something like this in their breaks. It's always welcome.

PEART. What about that girl we heard about?

TEACHER. Ah - ?

PEART. What was her - Lyn, she was called, I think.

TEACHER. Lyn - the - oh, yes. Not very good material, I think. She - I don't mind telling you - has proved a little burdensome to some of the teachers. Very little discipline.

PEART. Was she the -

TEACHER. Some of her - sorry.

PEART. Sorry.

TEACHER. Some of her behaviour in class has not been tasteful.

PEART. Teachers disliked it, did they?

TEACHER. She was selling clothes in one - taking off - I believe - and selling items of clothing during a class.

Fortunately she's not popular - and the others, I think, have all seen her more as example of what not to follow than -

PEART. Older than the others, is she?

TEACHER. She's - yes - one of the oldest.

> (LOUYS enters.
>
> He confers with BRAATOY.
>
> Moments elapse.
>
> PEART drinks.
>
> BIRGER whispers to ING-BRITT.
>
> Some time elapses)

BRAATOY. This is Louys.

> (LOUYS looks about.
>
> Some time elapses.
>
> They confer)

TEACHER. You had heard of this assembly they plan to hold?

PEART. Bit of trouble brewing?

TEACHER. Certain of the teachers, actually, had anticipated some trouble.

> The younger pupils have been restive: some problems.
>
> I'm shortly to be called for a meeting to discuss this in fives - so I think I should leave now.
>
> I enjoyed the fruit.
>
> (She goes)

BRAATOY. Ah -

> Just a moment - I wanted a few words with -

PEART. I call her back?

BRAATOY. That's - no - no, that's all right. I'll go -

Can I leave Louys here? This is Louys.

(He goes. PEART and LORETTE follow)

BIRGER. Hello.

This is Birger: I'm Ing-Britt.

No: other way round.

LOUYS. Which is Ing-Britt?

ING-BRITT. I'm Ing-Britt.

LOUYS. I'm glad to see you.

BIRGER. I'm Birger.

LOUYS. Hello.

BIRGER. That's the horse.

HORSE. I'm delighted, Louys. It is Louys? Yes, I've
been questioning Ing-Britt on terms and faces of this
situation.

Bit of a problem.

LOUYS. What have you found? Anything of note?

HORSE. Filled a couple of sides of notepaper. Show them
to you sometime, if you like.

LOUYS. I'd be glad to see them now.

HORSE. Haven't got them on me, unfortunately. Believe
that teacher, what's her name, took them away with
her when she left.

LOUYS. In that case we can see them another time.

HORSE. I - perhaps you can tell me something of your

own circumstances. Like to enlarge my horizons a
little, you know: time to time.

Why don't you have a seat?

SANDIE. My name's Sandie.

LOUYS. I'm Louys.

SANDIE. I don't think you should talk too much with the
horse. He's confused. He's got most of his facts wrong
- and I don't think you'll find him very good company.

LOUYS. Seems enterprising enough. What's he supposed
to be doing?

HORSE. I'll have these files over in a moment.

LOUYS. Would you like a sweet?

SANDIE. Love one.

Nice wooden box.

LOUYS. Very old, in fact.

SANDIE. Grey - that's an odd colour for sweets.

LOUYS. They're quite good - improve the circulation.

SANDIE. The grey colour's a good idea. I might not have
had it otherwise. Aren't you having one?

LOUYS. No, I'm not having one now.

SANDIE. Your circulation's good enough, is it?

BIRGER. Can I have one?

SANDIE. Did you guess that mine was bad, or just have an
instinct?

LOUYS. Here.

BIRGER. Lovely: colour, I mean.

(She eats)

Taste good, too.

Sort of -

SANDIE. Mushroomy taste -

BIRGER. No, I - not...

I once went into an old room that smelt like this tastes - Powdery smell. Did you say they were good for circulation?

LOUYS. Quite good.

BIRGER. Mine's all right anyway, I think.

(She eats)

Nice flavour.

Ing-Britt - that one's - quieter than the others, but faktisk our leader.

SANDIE. Birger is second-in-command.

BIRGER. At times we wear arm-bands - red ones - for our seniority.

What's happened to the - oh, he's reading.

ING-BRITTA. Are you from Pine's? Since you spoke to Braatoy, I thought you'd probably come about water-repairs - something like that.

LOUYS. No - .

ING-BRITT. You obviously had some trouble bridging the floes.

Shoes are worn.

LOUYS. Yes - I'm not a good walker - they went through early.

ING-BRITT. We can give you slippers if you like. We can dry those for you.

LOUYS. They're not very wet.

ING-BRITT. You may as well: it'll air them anyway.

Can you move over? (To HORSE)

HORSE. Ing-Britt - I've discovered a fresh reference - something I'd like you to verify sometime, if you would.

ING-BRITT. Just a moment.

(She brings slippers)

Can you help him change, Sandie?

SANDIE. Sit down.

LOUYS. They're not that wet, but I - thank you.

ING-BRITT. I found this too.

(She reveals it)

BIRGER. A musical box.

ING-BRITT. Handle's been degaged.

BIRGER. It's -

Lovely sort of panelling on it -

Here's part of a crow... a lion's foot.

SANDIE. Can I see?

ING-BRITT. One of these objects that were meant to sain problems of the mind.

BIRGER. Problems actualised into a kind of -

ING-BRITT. This to sain or heal the imperfections or tensions some people have to existence.

SANDIE. What a colour.

All the...

(LOUYS has risen)

LOUYS. Does it play anything?

ING-BRITT. They usually don't.

(She goes to a table)

SANDIE. Can I see?

(ING-BRITT plays a single note)

BIRGER. One: try it the other way.

Yes: the same.

LOUYS. I'm interested in the markings.

ING-BRITT. Have a look at it.

(She gives it)

LOUYS. The -

Are these things letters, or -

ING-BRITT. They're parts of figures: drawings.

LOUYS. What is the design?

HORSE. Is there something there that might interest me?

SANDIE. Probably an old woodland design - or might be abstract.

HORSE. Come to think of it, might be something I could help to clarify.

ING-BRITT. Can you take charge of the horse? I don't want him to intrude if it can be avoided.

BIRGER. Come on, Matthew, I'll show you a new game.

HORSE. Always glad to break fresh ground, Birger.

What is this game?

(TIBS enters and leaves)

LOUYS. Green markings. Are these likely to represent formes?

SANDIE. I had a dream recently - actually when I was waiting for a milk-urn to be filled.

There was water in it - rooms full of water and you had to walk over the - walk round the walls to get from one room to - where there was just a space - to another. There was a band playing in one room. Sorry, I've knocked your -

LOUYS. Doesn't matter.

SANDIE. Of animals - an animal-band. Couldn't get to it. Though I could hear them: it became a - no, then there was a babe, poised at the edge of huge blades of grass that - or green wheat - that were being - in a field - being cut by a huge machine. The babe was poised at the edge, no matter where they were cutting.

Then it became a passage - or series of passageways, very straight - long - all leading into one another. In one of the caves - sort of long passage-like caves - some groups of children, with sort of heads as turnips, turnip-heads - but groups of different colours - some dark brown - other purple and green - all with kind of - sprouting stuff - turnip-stuff - in their hair.

LOUYS. Any special feelings or anything, in the dream?

SANDIE. Nothing - no - nothing special - I was fairly happy just going around from one place to another.

Earlier in the dream there was a blind harper - but I don't remember how he - : he fitted in somewhere, I'm not sure where.

LOUYS. Do you think it could have anything to do with our finding this box?

SANDIE. How could it?

I'd like to show you some of the formations, if you'd -

(TIBS enters)

Hello, Tibs.

TIBS. Hello -

SANDIE. I'm just going to show some of the formations of my dream, and the colour effects.

Could you just stand there? There.

Birger - do you think you could help?

BIRGER. I'm showing this horse how to hold a pen.

HORSE. Perhaps both do something to help this lady - Sandie, isn't it? Or is it?

SANDIE. I don't want the horse distracting: he's generally of more value on the sidelines.

TIBS. Have any of you got food?

HORSE. More value?

ING-BRITT. An orange at the back of that cupboard.

TIBS. This one?

HORSE. On what sidelines?

TIBS. There's been a crisis - a child was tortured and its words taken down.

I can't find this orange.

ING-BRITT. It's at the back.

TIBS. I've looked at the back.

(ING-BRITT goes to the cupboard)

BIRGER. What happens when the child was tortured?

SANDIE. The teacher took the last one. I just want to show you a feature of this dream.

TIBS. One of the children was being tortured, and they took down its words, all it said.

ING-BRITT. The teacher must have taken the last one.

Was it revealing?

HORSE. I'm trying to interpret a remark Sandie recently made to me.

TIBS. I don't think it was much use to them - simply occupied their time. Some of them drew its face during the act: others collected its blood in a golden casket.

Apparently right at the end it had a baby.

BIRGER. At the end?

TIBS. Under the stress of the torture it finally gave birth - to a young rabbit. It was in pain, come to the end of its tether - the only thing it could do was have a babe.

The creature's now galloping around - not a care in the world.

SANDIE. Did you see this, or just hear a report?

TIBS. I heard a fairly good report.

Have you got anything now the last orange has gone?

BIRGER. It sounds very inaccurate: a child doesn't give birth -

and a - and anyway I've read that torture - that you can't have a child at the end of torture - only before or during.

TIBS. It's authenticated. Braatoy will tell you.

Are these biscuits there?

LOUYS. I'm rather interested to learn more about this. I'd heard a little of the children's aims - but heard they were spontaneous - hadn't been recorded.

TIBS. I'll tell you more when I've eaten. Watching a display like that gives you a strong need for food.

HORSE. Quite sound, I'm sure. All support Tibs over that. 'Tibs' is right, isn't it?

LOUYS. I've got some stored away - a little. I'll be happy to share with you.

HORSE. Just what's wanted, Louys. I'll certainly support.

BIRGER. I've done all I can - he's too frisky to keep under control.

I tried to teach him art: triangles - how good designs are based on triangles.

LOUYS. Blue powder.

HORSE. An original idea: taste any good?

I dare say you carry it around with you.

BIRGER. How did you get hold of it?

HORSE. Don't mind tasting a shot myself.

LOUYS. I've been told it induces visions, but there's -

I've always found it keeps my vision normal - see the right objects at the right time.

That chair, for instance.

(JANIE enters)

JANIE. There's been a delightful new event: a child roasted, and its words taken down.

TIBS. Janie.

SANDIE. That's Janie, one of the children.

HORSE. Actually, Janie - I heard of this - be very happy if you'd confirm it: like to get the picture straight.

JANIE. Who's the horse?

Hello, Auntie.

BIRGER. I'm not your auntie.

JANIE. Hello, Auntie Birger.

Yes. I was there. I helped set the - set the burners.

I've found a drum.

BIRGER. That's an old music-box we found.

JANIE. Yes, the child's name was Rodney. I've got a piece of his -

Doesn't work.

I've got a piece of his flesh. Turned blue.

BIRGER. Janie, that's revolting. You'll have to excuse her.

JANIE. The kid squawked - made a - made every noise you could think of - and there was a -

BIRGER. Don't annoy these people - they're friends.

JANIE. There was a terrific climax: leave me alone.

BIRGER. Why don't you sit down?

JANIE. I'm going to in a minute. I just want to show the horse a trick.

HORSE. I'm impressed, Birger, by the spirit of this little one.

Don't mind telling you that.

BIRGER. Don't romp, Janie.

HORSE. Taken my pad - why -

JANIE. Let's see what the horse has written.

Who can read?

HORSE. I'd rather you returned that, Janie. Contains a number of things I'd prefer to -

(JANIE leaps on a chair)

Can you retrieve it? Birger, I'd be grateful -

BIRGER. Nothing we can do when she's in this mood: she'll relax soon.

JANIE. Number one: the children have stolen several of the arm-bands that Miss Petersen locked in the chalk-cupboard.

BIRGER. I didn't think she can read: she can't, can she?

JANIE. Number two: one of the youngest ones, Michael, was not allowed coffee when he went to the kitchens.

BIRGER. She can't read?

TIBS. She's inventing. Janie, keep your voice down.

JANIE. Sh, I'm holding a seminar.

Tibs - sit - on the floor, please.

Sandie, next to him. Birger -

BIRGER. She's got amazing control.

JANIE. We're going to have a seminar on the horse's proposals. Birger - behind them, sitting.

BIRGER. I don't mind falling into her schemes. Her proposals are often energetic.

JANIE. That's right: behind.

Now, the horse. What's your name, horse - where are your manners?

SANDIE. His name's Matthew.

JANIE. On the floor then, Matthew. Quick as a wink - no whispering.

SANDIE. I should do it if I were you, Matthew: it will be over quickly.

JANIE. Come on, Matt.

HORSE. I'll admit I'm hardly used to this sort of -

She's asking us to form -

BIRGER. Come on, it'll be better for you. I'll give you some extra information if you do.

HORSE. Think I've hurt my ankle: yes.

JANIE. Come on, Mr Horse - don't dawdle, get into place.

Birger - make sure he's well in position.

BIRGER. I'm doing what I can.

JANIE. Give him a sweetie. That's right.

(BIRGER has given him a comfit)

Now, Mr Horse -

We'll begin.

Mr Horse - explain yourself - on page two of your memorandum - sit still, no fidgeting -

TIBS. You can understand the sort of attention she has in class.

JANIE. On page two - the following. Janie was put on a large pane of glass, made slippery with soap, and made to run across it.

What d'you mean by that? Defend your interest.

HORSE. I'm - seem to have lost my nerve: any of you help me?

BIRGER. Just say something to her that you think would please her.

SANDIE. (Whispers)

JANIE. No whispering, Sandie - Birger.

BIRGER. Sorry, Miss.

JANIE. That's better. Matthew - your answer's awaited.

(BIRGER whispers)

HORSE. When I wrote it, I was speaking in fanciful terms, not -

What?

Not as a - recommendation.

That's correct, is it?

JANIE. Thank you.

Next question.

First, Tibs, put that book away.

TIBS. Certainly.

(He puts away an imaginary book, having marked the place)

JANIE. Now, a second question.

What's that, Sandie?

SANDIE. The - I thought I heard the sound of a child crying.

JANIE. Where?

(She leaps off her chair, goes to the door)

BIRGER. Might be one of the Werthers, do you think?

JANIE. False alarm.

(She returns to the chair)

Question two. You said, in your notebook, that: a little boy, Godfrey, was locked in a sack containing moths.

He was allowed out occasionally for a drink.

What do you mean by that statement?

TIBS. One thing we were all hoping to ask you, Janie - the teacher was talking about Lyn just now - you know Lyn - what's your view of her activities?

JANIE. Right, Tibs, put your question.

TIBS. That was the question.

JANIE. Who'll answer that - Birger?

BIRGER. I can't answer it: it was your opinion that was wanted.

JANIE. I'm -

What was the question again?

TIBS. I'll put it more simply: the teacher was discussing Lyn - you know - one of the older girls - the one who wears tuile - she objected to her on the following grounds. Firstly - she never changes her clothes, always wears the same dress. Secondly - she has her own ideas about behaviour in class, - and also, she holds private meetings in a damp cave under that large rubbish site. The teachers haven't been invited to these.

JANIE. They should have asked for proper invitations.

BIRGER. The teacher thought her morals weren't good.

JANIE. Most of us consider her the most respectable one in the class.

Next.

(Some moments elapse.

JANIE leaves the chair)

Have you got something I can drink?

SANDIE. Will orange juice do?

JANIE. When the first child, Godfrey, was tortured, it wasn't that bad because in between pain sessions he was subjected to intense pleasure. This is cold.

LOUYS. What form did the pleasure take?

(The TEACHER enters)

TEACHER. I - goodness -

JANIE. Watch out - I'm going to get her.

(She runs at the teacher)

TEACHER. Birger: this creature's - can you -

(She avoids JANIE)

JANIE. Now I'll get you. What did you say about my best friend?

TEACHER. Now, dearie. Tibs, can you prevent the poor dear? I'm afraid she'll do damage.

TIBS. Otu mbe nanya ya isi, ukwu.

JANIE. Okwu ahu we n'ukwa n'elu inyinya-ibu, na nna-ya ka o neje ije ala.

TEACHER. What a - yes - a ferocious creature. Glad you've got her under control. I'll just sit down, if I may.

TIBS. I admire your pluck, Janie - but I don't think you should assail the teacher.

JANIE. I know something about her which none of you do, and I'll tell you in a moment. Let me go.

TIBS. Promise you won't strike her?

JANIE. Promise.

(TIBS releases JANIE.

She pauses as she passes the TEACHER, but goes and sits down in a corner)

LOUYS. Can I suggest you - if you want to pacify her - you might give us some of your views on teaching.

TEACHER. Some of - ?

LOUYS. Some of the techniques of your teaching. Obviously
you have several: techniques of silencing a child in
class, for example.

TEACHER. I'm not entirely certain I have your meaning,
Louys.

(They discuss)

HEN. I'm coming across what I think may prove to be a
discovery.

TIBS. Tibs, don't pull that bench to pieces.

JANIE. I'm writing my name on it: have to do it with my
nails. Jane, Janie, and the date, in full, as well as
the moon's quarter.

TEACHER. I believe I've grasped Louys's meaning,
children - and it's a - seems to be a - quite an
attractive one.

I'll discuss class-room techniques.

LOUYS. I'll just make sure there's no one at the -

No one listening.

(He does so)

Right.

TEACHER. First - Ah, I've dropped my book.

SANDIE. Here you are.

TEACHER. Thank you. First of all - whether children
should be permitted to eat in class. My answer to that
- very definitely no.

But there are exceptions - and we find one of these
where the father has returned, recently, with a large

catch of fish - the children are obliged to eat the - eat it - eat the - for him.

(The HORSE makes a note)

HORSE. Think we're all pleased with that answer.

TEACHER. Second question: how children should sit in class - and whether liberties should be permitted.

JANIE. What's the moon's phase?

TEACHER. Children should, in general, hold both desks on hands - their head a little tilted forward - pencil in right hand and slate in left.

Eyes should be firmly on the teacher.

JANIE. I'm getting tired of this. Anyone got the moon's declination or phase?

TEACHER. Tibs, I wonder - could you pacify the little creature?

TIBS. I'll try to, ma'am, but she's slippery.

JANIE. Come and pacify me, Tibs. I won't resist.

TEACHER. Third question: the teacher-pupil relationship.

BIRGER. Wait a moment - the turkeys are rising.

TEACHER. What - ? Birger - ?

JANIE. You're jealous of the pupils because they -

TIBS. Settle down, Janie, - here's something nice for you to look at.

TEACHER. Now, Janie, you must address the teacher pleasantly, you know.

BIRGER. Turkeys are rising, all over the valley.

TEACHER. Must have made a mistake, Birger. Turkeys?

BIRGER. Rising all over the valley - millions.

TEACHER. What d'you mean exactly by 'rising'?

HORSE. Must say - intrigued to witness this new sight of Birger's.

TEACHER. Personally, I'm not happy with the -

BIRGER. A moment - a moment of complete silence: it's only then that the - in extreme silence - that the turkeys can rise - millions.

There - you see that mass of wings, and -

HORSE. A striking - striking event... must say, I -

BIRGER. And the - then, a very slight sound, hardly notices, but the entire place falls in with it.

You see it - collapsing beautifully. Beautiful.

HORSE. Happening as she says. Unqualified performance.

TEACHER. Birger, I can't believe the - that this is - you must simply recall some of it.

HORSE. Description was accurate, as far as I could tell, Florence. Can't say I think you should make her modify.

TEACHER. What was your view, Sandie?

SANDIE. I'd say - I'd say it was the impression, more than the thing itself. It was spectacular.

TEACHER. I hardly think - ah.

Wonder what the children would think of this?

Feels very peculiar, I must say.

(She adjusts her hairnet)

LOUYS. What of the third section - to do with little rewards and punishments for children, wasn't it?

TEACHER. Rewards - ah - .

BIRGER. Yes, I'm sorry for the interruption.

SANDIE. Sorry.

HORSE. Found some truth in that. I'll see you afterwards about that, Birger.

BIRGER. Sh.

HORSE. Left me a new man. Yes.

TEACHER. Rewards for children, and when these should be offered - let me see now, - yes.

(She scrutinizes her paper)

I -

I rather think - ah - Sandie will answer this one.

SANDIE. Me? I - well -

What was the question again - must have -

LOUYS. Whether children - whether children should be rewarded.

SANDIE. Rewarded for -

HEN. I've discovered - I've come across what will probably turn out to be the answer here.

TEACHER. Sandie's answering. I think Sandie's going to answer this one.

SANDIE. Rewarding -

HEN. This is the answer to a much more important question. Explains the children's - explains the entire attitude of the children.

TEACHER. Go on, Sandie.

LOUYS. No, I -' no, I think the hen is probably on to a more important -

(He rises)

TEACHER. I dare say you -

TIBS. I think we should hear this, Florence.

HEN. I'll have it into the light.

(The group leaves the TEACHER and surrounds the HEN)

It's to do with octaves and cycles, and it quotes the case of - don't push.

LOUYS. Don't pen her in - let her have some light.

HEN. Apparently this arose from the time that Michael was sent -

JANIE. I want to see, I -

(She tries to see the book, but fails)

Why do you always -

TIBS. Give her some room - other she can't read.

HEN. Michael was sent out of the class for disobedience, and the following memorandum was - was drafted. First, children were to be reckoned into five cycles - according to mental ability, handicraft, aptitude, leadership. Then they're given endurance tests: told to face the teachers for five minutes without flinching. The higher -

the higher - I can't see if - the higher cycle defined by the children's normal attitude to their teachers during an average lesson.

JANIE. Much more interesting is the time Michael broke into the gym when the girls were changing, with a crowd of - and Lyn was there, and she organised a -

TIBS. I don't think you should do this just now: Maudie's discovered something that may bear on the situation.

HEN. Under the second heading: those who fail the first octave-test take lessons out of doors - they are read long extracts from adventure and other tales and told to formulate their own opinions. The intelligent ones are permitted to chart the progress of the class, as regards spelling and general aptitude.

JANIE. She's got no sense of what's important. She's trying to deprive us of our right to play in playtime. She's got - I hate you - get - she's got no right - go away.

TEACHER. Tibs, I don't think you should berate the poor one.

TIBS. I'm only trying to prevent her hurting you.

JANIE. She's the only one that likes me.

(She embraces the Teacher)

TEACHER. Ah - my net: too much latitude.

TIBS. Try and leave the teacher alone, Janie. You're - and -

JANIE. She likes me - and it's your fault that... get off.

(She wrestles with TIBS)

HEN. Meanwhile Michael reaches the kitchens. He runs in: cook's preparing broth -

TEACHER. Now - friends. You'll break a -

HEN. He's offered a taste. Do you see the picture? There's a caption - I can't quite -

BIRGER. The cook says: 'supper will soon be ready, Michael. Do you want a sniff of this?' 'Yes, I'd love it' - that's Michael's reply.

SANDIE. He's taking it.

BIRGER. No - it's too hot: he's -

SANDIE. Given it back to the cook -

JANIE. You were never on the side of the children: you're just watching and - all you want is -

SANDIE. Asking permission if they can hold assembly there?

HORSE. In the kitchens? Impressed - impressed by the amount you can extract from the - . As for me - eyes aren't what they were.

JANIE. I saw you in Angela's bedroom - Angela told me - all the children know - you've been -

HEN. I think you've misinterpreted. None of that last part is included in the text.

BIRGER. Then what's he doing here, then?

HEN. Where?

(BRAATOY enters)

BRAATOY. Children have been on the roof.

JANIE. Tibs has been pestering me: he's been forcing me to reveal secrets about you - twisting my arm and things.

SANDIE. Braatoy's come.

112

BRAATOY. Come, I can't believe that.

HORSE. I was impressed - and I hope that later we may be able to confirm a little of this - possibly over some soup and rolls.

JANIE. Teacher will confirm what I've said.

TEACHER. I -

BRAATOY. Don't trouble, Florence. You're required by a class. Class-leader recently informed me. They'll be attending as usual.

TEACHER. That means the - I'll have to -

BRAATOY. Janie, perhaps you can take her.

JANIE. Yes: she's my friend. Come on, Auntie.

(PEART appears)

SANDIE. If we put that away now there may be a chance of bringing out the news.

JANIE. Come on, Florence. Don't be afraid. Got your things?

She's not as brisk as she used to be.

BRAATOY. Been enjoying yourself, Janie?

JANIE. I did nearly everything I wanted to do, plus some other things which I didn't mind doing. Oh.

TEACHER. Come along, now, dearie. Say goodbye to Braatoy.

JANIE. Goodbye. I'll be seeing you again soon.

PEART. Hen been behaving itself?

HORSE. Quiet as a mouse: hasn't spoken actually.

BRAATOY. I'll tell Peter about your scheme.

(JANIE and the TEACHER leave)

We'll - Excuse me now: we'll be on some further systems.

Birger -

BIRGER. Anything I can do, Braatoy?

BRAATOY. I've - yes - I've just missed my coffee, and if you could run along down to the kitchens you might find a cup for me.

BIRGER. I'll certainly do that. Can you keep the hen occupied?

BRAATOY. I'd be very sorry to go without it.

SANDIE. I think so, if she's steady.

BIRGER. All right.

(She leaves)

BRAATOY. Well, Louys - fancy I rather liked that report of yours.

LOUYS. I'm glad to hear that.

Which report do you mean?

BRAATOY. Ah - I'm none too sure now. Was it the one on colour-grouping - the grouping of colour-cycles?

LOUYS. Grouping? No, I don't think that was - I don't think that was one of mine.

BRAATOY. You know the one with his head in a grey and brown border - wing-markings -

Tail made up of a line of feathers -

LOUYS. Could have been - I'm not certain if -

BRAATOY. I'll try and show you - get you a copy if I can. Just now I must pay attention to this side of activities.

We'll - just a moment now.

PEART. Boss says - keep quiet. Stop chattering, Sandie.

SANDIE. Wasn't me.

BRAATOY. Now we'll - I'd like the action of -

if we can all assemble first.

Now: the action of finding an unexpected treasure. Peart, I'd like you in this.

PEART. Right.

BRAATOY. We'll have you in it. And Sandie.

SANDIE. What shall I do?

HORSE. Think I'll sit over here, Louys - get a better view of the proceedings.

LOUYS. Incidentally - can I just interrupt you for a moment, Braatoy, - was there any recent information of the children, or other information?

BRAATOY. There hasn't been anything much - the usual squabbles. Some maintain - and I'm not certain of their right to do so - that there's a scheme to build a marquee in case of a change of plan.

LOUYS. A marquee?

BRAATOY. In case the normal assembly is threatened by rain.

There was a - there was a flight of turkeys a short while ago.

HORSE. Yes, we heard something of the kind.

BRAATOY. You did? Yes. About a thousand turkeys decided it was time to leave. Flew up into the sky's teeth. Quite a spectacle for all of us.

LOUYS. Yes, Birger noted something like that.

BRAATOY. It was pretty.

Now, I must get on with this section, I think.

Sandie -

SANDIE. Hello.

BRAATOY. Sandie is the crouching nymph discovered in the hollow tree-trunk by - by the returning woodman.

SANDIE. Am I frightened, or just - or just hungry or something and waiting for someone to turn up, or got my wings broken or something?

BRAATOY. You're not alarmed. Haven't seen food in days - husband eaten by a stickleback - dragged under - you know the sort of thing.

SANDIE. And I'm crouching on a leaf.

BRAATOY. On the - in the trunk, yes.

Peart, - can you do the crouching, Sandie - Peart appears - axe slung over shoulder - marches home.

PEART. Where do I stand, Braatoy?

BRAATOY. You know the feeling of a homeward trek. Hunger in the belly - evening coming on. Birds beginning to chirrup - you find your - sorry.

SANDIE. That's all right.

(He trod on SANDIE's toe)

BRAATOY. Can you try - try the expression. You stand over there. Over - yes. Now for the expression.

HORSE. Amused by this: think it might offer a new trend.

BRAATOY. No - no, that's -

HORSE. If we're lucky - witness something quite new.

LOUYS. I'm not sure this hasn't been done before. But I'm struck by his authority.

BRAATOY. You're looking too - too wilted. Straighten up a little. It's the evening: flowers beginning to - dews falling.

Manage a smile?

(PEART does not smile)

Yes.

I see.

You can't - ah -

Sandie: apprehension on your visage. Very nice.

Yes, that's very - very - very effective, I must say. Yes.

Sorry.

That's quite an effective - effective - Quite an effective expression. Just let me see it from this angle.

(He squats.

BIRGER enters)

BIRGER. Coffee's here.

BRAATOY. Yes - I think we'll let that pass. Thank you,

Birger.

No trouble getting it, did you?

BIRGER. Nothing - none.

BRAATOY. Looks very nice.

(He stirs)

LOUYS. I've taken note of some of the actions. Others I'm not too sure of.

HORSE. What's the best indication of Peart's agility?

BRAATOY. Birger - you might take over part of this episode, while I'm sipping the - this mixture.

Peart's returning. Sandie's in one of those sort of - you know how where a tree has roots - those little pool things - she's in one.

BIRGER. Yes. All right, then. Peart moves with a light step - three paces from the - from where I'm standing. Arms down.

BRAATOY. No: no, the arms are for his instruments: his axe, axe and things like that.

BIRGER. For his axe: all right.

Now - three light paces - you step in that direction. Pause at the base of the tree-trunk, facing - in that direction: there.

PEART. Which direction of the -

BIRGER. In that - in that direction. All right. Let's start it.

You walk - yes.

(PEART performs the action)

BIRGER. He - yes, that's all right. Not too bad.

Now - he sees the creature - and instantly - out she
skips - sort of well, I never, she's out and away, and -
Peart two paces to the side: Birger - I mean Sandie -
a pace sideways, sideways and - still crouching - then
straighten up to half - to a sort of half-crouch. Hops
back, still looking at him. Peart puts his weapons
down - whew! exhaustion, excitement, etc.

PEART. Can you repeat that?

BRAATOY. I think -

(He clears his throat)

I think you're too anxious to have him jump. That's
the first point, and also - also Sandie the fay can't
hop sideways with such - no, she should shoot up - as
if to grab a twig, or branch, then fall on the ground,
broken. A gasp - a moment of horror - then she
stumbles back.

BIRGER. All right. Like that, then.

(The action is performed)

Peart, you should be more flexible in your arm-
movements. You seemed to be hitting her - almost. I
mean, when you, when you put your things on the
ground.

PEART. I don't want to get her off her guard.

BIRGER. No. Perhaps more to the right of -

(She adjusts her position)

Or - .

BRAATOY. Now, Lorette. Can you systematize a little?
Birger can - can sit down if she wishes, though don't
degage your interest. Sandie, we'll use you. Peart
can rest.

PEART. That was all right, was it?

BRAATOY. Louys, perhaps we might use you. Would you like to do a little?

SANDIE. Can I sit down a moment?

LOUYS. I'd like to.

(He comes forward)

HORSE. Birger - I'd like to try you on something.

BIRGER. What?

HORSE. A new device I've learned. Quite out of the blue.

(He wrestles with some papers. BIRGER watches the action)

BRAATOY. He front him - falls he the - strikes he the: eji kwa ahihia anakpo iwele ma-obu uriom ebu azu. Mbe anasa ahihia ahu na miri, azu o bula nke di na miri ahu ganwu.

HORSE. Onye a bula nke bu onye-anya-uku.

BRAATOY. Louys has taken a book from the shelf.

Sandie approaches him.

LORETTE. All right. Louys there. Sandie over there.

BRAATOY. Keep - don't keep them too far apart.

LORETTE. Nearer apart - nearer together. Louys a little in front. Takes a book from the shelf - the shelf about level with your neck -

Sandie has seen him. She comes up, three paces fast, then two slower as she - as she - she makes the charge.

Louys, infuriated, throws the book at her: throws it at her face. Sandie kneels down to pick it up - Louys shocked at what he has done, and then you -

BRAATOY. That's - that's promising enough: shall we try the action? Birger - I should be glad of any comments.

BIRGER. It's a rewarding action.

LORETTE. All right, then. Louys takes a book. Now Sandie.

Three. Now two. Make your charge.

Louys, infuriated.

No. No, that won't do.

BIRGER. Get him to squint a little as he does it.

LORETTE. It's something to do with your face: what you register.

(Some moments elapse)

BRAATOY. Think of it more from his point of view than tell him what to do.

BIRGER. His eyes should open wider.

LORETTE. Try and open your eyes wider.

(LOUYS is unable to perform this action)

HORSE. Impressive effect, Louys - don't mind telling you.

LORETTE. Sh.

BRAATOY. Try and keep the horse out of it, if you can.

HORSE. Yes, I will.

(Some time elapses)

LORETTE. Throw the book at her.

(LOUYS makes a brief action)

BIRGER. Harder, and throw it at her.

LORETTE. Throw it harder.

(LOUYS does not perform the action.

Some moments elapse)

Oh dear.

Oh, well - Sandie to be shocked - bend to pick up the book.

(SANDIE performs the action)

Now, give it to him.

(SANDIE offers the book. LOUYS does not accept)

SANDIE. Take it: I can't -

LORETTE. He doesn't seem to want to take it. What shall I do, Braatoy?

BRAATOY. Come on, Louys - be responsive - a simple action, you know.

(Some moments elapse)

BIRGER. Try giving it to him with the other side. The other side of the book.

SANDIE. Won't make any difference.

LORETTE. I'm sure that won't make any difference.

SANDIE. There.

(She offers the book. LOUYS does not accept it.

Several moments elapse.

Someone offstage calls: 'Martin, did you see what happened to the child in green?'

Another voice: 'Think the teacher's taken it. '

First voice: 'Oh, that means the - . '

Some moments elapse)

LORETTE. I don't know what to suggest. Perhaps Sandie can do something by herself.

SANDIE. I'm strained.

(She goes to sit down)

BRAATOY. Hard to know what course to take, really. Dare say someone will come up with something.

Birger - I enjoyed your coffee very much.

BIRGER. I'm glad you did, Braatoy.

BRAATOY. I hope there'll be more like it.

HORSE. I've a brief number of questions for you, Braatoy: think you might be able to help on a few points.

BRAATOY. I'd like to, Matthew, but just now I'm a little tired, really. Don't feel - well, I know I could answer them, but, in my present state, I don't suppose I'd give you very interesting or vivid answers.

HORSE. That's all right.

I liked the work I've just seen - found it stimulating. Some of these new techniques, you know, I've fought shy of. But these - well - these provided a measure of interest.

BRAATOY. I'm glad to hear you got something out of them.

HORSE. Another thing I'd like to ask you -

(GJORDA enters)

GJORDA. A child - a child shut itself in a lift, and has been going up and down - nothing anyone can do to stop it, though there are hordes of people waiting by the exits.

BRAATOY. What about the safety button?

HORSE. That's Gjorda, isn't it?

LORETTE. Yes.

GJORDA. The child - they couldn't do anything about it: it grinned in the most peculiar way each time it passed a group of people. I've brought you these.

BRAATOY. What are they?

GJORDA. I'm not sure. It's from the corridor.

(She takes a musical pipe from the box and sits down.

ING-BRITT enters and leaves)

HORSE. I'd be glad of any more information you could offer. I've filled -

(He searches)

BRAATOY. A chance of taking the...

and...

PEART. (Inaudible)

BRAATOY. After a while they felt that none of his... (inaudible)

PEART. The stoat had found that...

... after...

BRAATOY. Hard to work out.

LOUYS. What are you looking for?

HORSE. Trying to persuade - trying to convince this girl of more information.

LORETTE. I've read most of his screed, and I don't understand it.

LOUYS. Does it deal with the changing of lights - patterning of them?

LORETTE. Not so far as I can gather. But then I'm...

(She yawns)

Oh.

(She yawns again)

LOUYS. I can see they had some difficulty in attempting it. Have they recovered?

(ING-BRITT enters.

She speaks to BRAATOY.

After some moments he leaves with PEART. TIBS, LORETTE, LOUYS and the HEN also leave)

ING-BRITT. Hello, Beri.

BIRGER. Gjorda's come and no one's asked her anything about what she's brought or anything.

ING-BRITT. Is the parcel from the children?

BIRGER. I think so.

GJORDA. Yes. I brought it a little time ago. Most of it's surplus.

(She reveals one item)

ING-BRITT. A black dress.

GJORDA. No, it's a - an ordinary piece of cloth.

(She holds it up)

BIRGER. A new sight.

(She goes to the window)

Coloured rain!

GJORDA. It's the orange rain: they predicted it.

BIRGER. Orange, yes.

ING-BRITT. They expected that, did they?

GJORDA. They thought it might happen.

BIRGER. What's so different about orange rain? What's special about it?

GJORDA. It's very light - and its texture is different - it's a bit spongy. Some of it floats upward.

BIRGER. Yes, there's a bit here.

(She tastes a bit with her finger)

Rather nice.

ING-BRITT. Has the horse been seen to?

BIRGER. No one was sure what happened to him. They finally went out. I think he's all right. I'm not sure if Braatoy found him.

(The HORSE leaves)

ING-BRITT. What of your recent experiences?

GJORDA. I was looking after some of the children. I was at a seminar - a sort of child-seminar just now - and one child started leaping on a chair - asking as many questions as it could.

ING-BRITT. They answered, did they?

GJORDA. Some of them did - if they could. There's a very nice, sweet one - Rodney - orange hair: he's my favourite of them. Straight orange hair. He had a good idea and they've taken it.

BIRGER. I heard they'd put up a marquee in the event of rain.

GJORDA. Yes, their assembly. They've got to hold their assembly, you see. That was a fine one.

BIRGER. The trees are almost uprooted.

Waving the -

There's a mauve slave walking under one of them. Wonderful colour - wonderful... Look.

GJORDA. A kind of mauve.

ING-BRITT. Bright mauve.

BIRGER. Walking - superb ease - got a bit of the - bit of the marquee in his hand.

GJORDA. I'll tell you something about what happened in the gardens. Marcellino, one of the littlest boys, was walking, seeing the - seeing the flowers and things.

Hears some calls coming from a shed - went to it - puts his ear to it.

Peart's in there: and one of the youngest girls is in there.

BIRGER. What was the - ?

ING-BRITT. Did he report it?

GJORDA. He wasn't sure what had happened. No one was. But Peart always had a terrific thing about very young children. An absolute terrific thing. He hated being without them for long.

BIRGER. He was always praising one of the youngest ones - Mary.

GJORDA. The brown-haired one - she's got eyes that are a real mystery. Peart said - her eyes flavour the rest of her - they are her flavour.

ING-BRITT. He was often cryptic. You shouldn't attach a lot of importance to some of his remarks.

GJORDA. I don't.

ING-BRITT. He was - he was also keen on trying the delight-pain thing on the children. Alternation.

BIRGER. The rain's not so good now.

ING-BRITT. He'd stretch them out and - oh, well.

I've got to go and get Monica from one of those rooms. I'll hear more from her.

GJORDA. She's sweet.

BIRGER. Yes, she's very sweet.

ING-BRITT. I like her - most of the things she does. She once wrapped seaweed round someone.

BIRGER. Thousands of turkeys.

ING-BRITT. What?

BIRGER. Rising from the -

GJORDA. What is it? Turkeys - ?

BIRGER. Thousands of turkeys are rising - Men are trying to restrain them. Absolutely filling the air.

ING-BRITT. I'm surprised they have enough to do that.

(She leaves)

GJORDA. I must say, I like the effect.

Reminds me of a prank of Rodney's. Quite a -

Quite a spectacle.

(She goes and fetches her pipe. Plays a few notes)

The seaweed occasion was in class. Teacher happened to start on a subject she didn't like - Monica didn't like. Next minute the boy in the row next to her was fronded in seaweed.

BIRGER. Did they discover what made her do it?

(PEART enters)

PEART. There's been orange rain. Lot of the children caught in it.

BIRGER. Yes, we saw it and enjoyed it.

PEART. Full thing - all over the place - fortunately, most people were within sight of shelter.

I was near a pillar myself.

(He stirs his drink)

Horse has left its doings. Uh - yes.

Any of you know anything about them?

They've been expecting the turkeys to rise shortly.

BIRGER. They've risen. You might still see them.

PEART. Any outside?

GJORDA. No - there are none left. They tried to hold them back, but none stayed.

PEART. Stayed - yes - when one - when one goes, all of
them go.

(He wanders)

Want something to do with my hands.

GJORDA. Have a look through some of these.

PEART. What are those?

GJORDA. I'm not sure. Someone just brought them in.

PEART. Not sure if I'll find what I'm looking for in this.

(He rummages)

GJORDA. Do you know how I could improve my playing on
this? It's got five holes, you see - but I can't even
get five sounds out of it.

BIRGER. Give me it a moment.

PEART. Revolting - something - something very
revolting about this pile.

(BIRGER plays a note)

Thought I was - thought I was discovering part of my
body stuffed in among the - among the stuff.

Birger - !

BIRGER. What's the matter?

PEART. Unhealthy flavour about this pile. Could you get
rid of it before the boss reappears. Had rather an
ugly feeling when delving into it. Got my hand greased.

BIRGER. I think I can see something crawling in it.

(She looks.

TIBS appears)

130

TIBS. There's been a panic. Anyone got soup?

Peart - boss has been looking for you.

BIRGER. What are they doing in the marquee?

TIBS. I think he wants your help in walking down a very wide flight of stairs.

PEART. Must be in trouble.

(He goes)

TIBS. Did I hear you say there was a bit of soup? No?

BIRGER. I'll see.

TIBS. Had to get rid of him. There have been some unhealthy reports of his behaviour. He was with a child in one of the sheds.

BIRGER. I don't think there is any.

GJORDA. It doesn't matter just being in a shed with a child.

TIBS. No - no, I know - But the child afterwards gave a long description - and the result wasn't rosy for Peart.

GJORDA. What sort of thing did it mention?

BIRGER. I can't find any soup here.

TIBS. Actually, I had my eyes on that babe, too. It was a rosy creature: good eyes. Nice pair of teeth.

BIRGER. I'll make you soup in this.

TIBS. Are these the horse's reports?

(He settles to read)

BIRGER. Gjorda, you remember when Braatoy sent me to

get some coffee?

GJORDA. Just before the last lot of - yes.

BIRGER. I went to the kitchens. One of the cooks was there - dead. And here's the odd thing: the remains - what was left of the coffee in a tin was so - sort of - covered, and sort of clotted up with blood that I couldn't use it.

GJORDA. How did you manage to bring up a cup? I remember he said he enjoyed it.

BIRGER. Found a - I was going around the kitchen - found some brown powder-paint - just a little, and mixed it with water. Brought it up - it was the right colour - he loved it.

GJORDA. Or pretended to.

BIRGER. Well, he said he liked it several times. So - either he liked it, or just pretended to.

TIBS. Can't say I'm amused by these reports. What do you girls think? Gjorda?

GJORDA. They're assembling: the marquee's gone up.

BIRGER. I had the idea they would the minute the marquee was finished.

GJORDA. The last mauve slave - a sweet boy - leaving the final pillar.

He's fantastically sweet.

BIRGER. Now people are entering it. I can't see very well.

GJORDA. I once had a long, wonderful discussion with him. Tried to give him pleasure. As much as I could of it.

BIRGER. Three children - curly - entering hand in hand.

(TIBS has found a crow's head in a corner. Now he

puts it on and begins to nose the girls)

TIBS. There's acute tension here.

GJORDA. I wish you wouldn't - it's rather frightening.

BIRGER. Don't do it, Tibs.

(TIBS bellows)

GJORDA. What's he trying to do?

BIRGER. He's changed his direction now: there's no let-up.

GJORDA. Is he trying to warn us?

BIRGER. Keep to the window.

(Some moments elapse)

He's ferreting.

GJORDA. How long will he do it for? Come on, Tibs. Stop this. Once, when I with children, Algy something this.

Will it be all right?

BIRGER. Ignore him - look out of the window.

GJORDA. I can't help thinking what he's doing.

BIRGER. He'll just ferret around a bit. Look, someone's bringing mats.

(TIBS bellows)

GJORDA. What does he mean by it?

BIRGER. Some children, running -

(TIBS removes the head)

TIBS. I'm not entirely happy with that.

BIRGER. Running away - without their -

TIBS. Had a moment of panic: thought I'd get myself out of it.

BIRGER. One of the children climbing out of the top.

TIBS. As soon as I stop, my imagination acutes.

He's got it - !

BIRGER. Don't attention him - D'you see that crawling creature? Sort of baby-thing.

TIBS. He's got the whole thing!

You can't have me!

Uh - the creature...

No, a moment of rest.

Back!

(He lies on the ground. ING-BRITT enters)

ING-BRITT. The hen's being plucked.

Hello, Gjorda.

GJORDA. Tibs has been having convulsions - fortunately enjoying a moment of respite.

ING-BRITT. I'm glad of that - the respite, I mean. The heat's been bad.

TIBS. I can't see the creature. I can feel him multiplying himself in the room.

ING-BRITT. Peart was killed.

BIRGER. Peart?

ING-BRITT. Fantastically quickly. Slivered up. Don't

134

think he felt much.

BIRGER. He put - he was quite all right when he was here last. That is, if - well.

GJORDA. I thought he was all right.

ING-BRITT. Come on, Tibs.

(She stands him up)

TIBS. I thought I had finally caught him. Did any of you see my papers?

ING-BRITT. And the last thing was - delight and pain, offered to a teacher. You might know that.

BIRGER. We heard something like that from Florence.

GJORDA. How much pain was there in connexion with the hen being plucked?

ING-BRITT. Several - well - several people left during it. During the experience. Thing went all right, really. Wasn't much pain.

GJORDA. I can just make out people moving slowly to and from the marquee. Very slow.

ING-BRITT. Tibs - Braatoy said he wanted to see you. He's by one of the large steel cauldrons.

TIBS. That means he wants me for an analysis.

ING-BRITT. Wants to see you soon, anyway.

TIBS. I'll take my papers.

(He collects a few of the HORSE's papers and leaves. BIRGER goes to pick up one of the papers.

She scans it.

Some moments elapse)

GJORDA. I wonder if this was done before or after the event.

BIRGER. Yes...

(Some moments elapse.

The HEN enters)

HEN. Peart's been plucked.

BIRGER. Plucked - ! Not -

Terrible. Did he have any pain?

HEN. Squealed a bit. You know that paper that I found?

BIRGER. Which?

HEN. The one that solved one of the range of problems. The one I read out. You don't remember it?

BIRGER. No.

HEN. The one I read out about Michael and the others - how they were involved - that sort of thing.

The one about them all sitting round a tree.

BIRGER. You mean Peart and the child in that shed?

HEN. No.

(LOUYS enters and leaves)

BIRGER. Well - I can't imagine what you mean. What shed?

GJORDA. They're putting up the seventh house: marriage has been proposed for some, and partnerships for the other.

BIRGER. Sh, the hen's trying to tell me something. What shed?

HEN. You know that long - rather - that wooden shed - rather a dark smell - sort of tar.

BIRGER. Yes, I know the one.

HEN. By the seventh arbour.

BIRGER. Yes, I know the one.

HEN. Peart was giving them a lesson there. And apparently it interested them much more - far more - than what the teachers had taught them.

BIRGER. What's this got to do with the story?

HEN. Apparently, very few children knew the pleasure they could give the teacher. They regarded pleasure as... well, having been given some pleasant toy, or something.

BIRGER. You mean, producing pleasure in the teacher was so - was so enjoyable to them that they didn't mind to what extent they gave it.

HEN. Pleasuring people and animals - yes.

BIRGER. But how does it - yes, I see. But how does it fit in with the Peart thing?

(PEART enters)

PEART. Getting pretty hot out there.

Did I hear you say earlier you had some soup?

BIRGER. I thought there was some. I can try if you like.

PEART. You're wanted, anyway.

BIRGER. What?

PEART. Braatoy said he wanted you: he was down by the stairs.

BIRGER. Said he wanted me?

PEART. I should get along: they're rounding some of them up.

BIRGER. Oh.

(She leaves the soup)

Perhaps the hen can prepare this. I'll see what I can do.

(She goes)

HEN. I'm afraid I've got no idea how to prepare soup, Peart.

PEART. Extraordinary thing was - this chicken - leaping around in the kitchen.

They'd started plucking it. Creature got away. Whole lot of people around, trying to catch it.

GJORDA. Do you want something special to eat? I'll try and prepare it if you do.

PEART. Eat? Well - got something in this bag.

Anyway. Thing was leaping around - spewing - actually spewing out vomit all over the place.

Golden vomit.

HEN. What reaction did they have?

PEART. Cooks and people were trying to collect the stuff as a souvenir.

(ING-BRITT enters)

ING-BRITT. A number of the pillars are down. Anyone heard anything?

HEN. Peart was telling us about the chicken.

ING-BRITT. I heard about that. Didn't believe most of it. Did you see Braatoy though?

PEART. Braatoy was down by some wide steps when I saw him - trying to get down them.

Not as steady as he used to be. I sent Birger to help him.

ING-BRITT. Why did you do that? Did he ask you to?

PEART. I couldn't see him very well: I was some way off - but his mouth kept opening and closing - seemed to be repeating some words. Thought Birger was the best person to help.

ING-BRITT. Don't think she's much chance of getting there. Stairs are broken through - you can hardly walk on them.

PEART. Got some meat here, if any of you are interested. Bit of chicken-leg.

HEN. I wouldn't mind having some.

(PEART produces meat from a bag)

PURITY
1966

Clannesse who so kyndly cowthe comende
And rekken up alle the resouns that ho by riht askez,
Fayre formes myht he fynde in forthering his speche,
And in the contrare, kark and combraunce huge.

CLANNESSE (Purity), 14th cent.

PURITY was first presented by the Manchester Drama Group at the Stables Theatre Club, Manchester, on 4th April 1969, with the following cast:

LORNA	Fiona Walker
JULIE	Katherine Barker
KERNITZ	Ewen Solon
FINN	Richard Howard
The play was directed by	Roger Tucker

(Darkened office. Projector at centre. JULIE sits facing front. LORNA stands by the projector)

JULIE. Ugh!

Poor little thing.

(Some moments elapse)

Who could want to see that?

LORNA. Thank God there's no sound track.

JULIE. Screaming his eyes out.

LORNA. Shall I turn it off?

(Some moments elapse)

JULIE. Is he dead?

LORNA. Fainted, I think.

Giving him an injection to wake him up.

JULIE. It's perverted.

LORNA. Finish.

(The film stops. LORNA turns the light on)

JULIE. Who'd want to see a thing like that?

(LORNA takes the reel from the projector and puts it on the side)

LORNA. I suppose just enjoy watching suffering. They don't have much feeling in their lives, so a spectacle of someone in pain gives them a thrill.

JULIE. Gives me the creeps.

LORNA. And a child pleases them even more.

(Some moments elapse)

JULIE. They might at least have left his clothes on.

I suppose some people just enjoy watching that sort of thing.

LORNA. Too late for inclusion.

JULIE. What will you do? Burn it?

LORNA. Send it back.

If they show it to children, then... Children wouldn't mind really. But afterwards might dream about it, or imagine it was happening to them. A child being operated on - I don't think that would scare them - but later... Their imagination's so clear...

JULIE. Time for coffee. Had three cups so far today. Three to the hour. K will be -

(She goes into the annexe. After a while she emerges. She stands, thinking, for some time. Sits down)

Letters.

(She doesn't move)

Itchy.

(She scratches her bosom)

Was going to tell you something. Forgotten.

What's happening to that lot there?

LORNA. Forgotten. Going back.

JULIE. What, all?

> Don't think I slept one moment last night. Kept
> thinking of the most stupid things. May have dozed off
> but I don't think I did.

LORNA. That will need a crate - get rid of. I'm surprised
we can't throw all that stuff away. There's a rule it
has to go back. It's the manufacturers' property.

JULIE. Returnable.

LORNA. Part of it will go on, but I don't know. Kernitz is
vague. I'll have to look through it. He gives you the
impression he...

> (She examines a pile of papers)

JULIE. Water's boiling.

> (She goes out. LORNA picks up a magazine and puts it
> down again. She sits at a table and opens a book)

JULIE. (Off) Anyway, K will...

> (Inaudible)

LORNA. Can't hear you.

> (JULIE re-enters holding a cup of coffee. She spills
> some onto her hand)

JULIE. Schmidt.

> Does K think it should be shown?

LORNA. The operation?

JULIE. What's his view?

LORNA. He doesn't have views.

JULIE. Um.

Too hot. Sodding coffee.

(She wipes a letter)

LORNA. Either it'll be shown or else it'll be banned.

(Some moments elapse)

JULIE. Did I turn the kettle off?

LORNA. Or else...

JULIE. Can't think yet. What day of the week is it? Dear Sir - I hate you.

LORNA. A film seems to get through without anyone taking a decision. Some sort of undefined thing. K never takes thought. Thing just happens.

And this is a censor's office.

JULIE. Oh, that reminds me.

(She sips coffee)

LORNA. Your last cup.

JULIE. K wants an assistant for the next doings.

LORNA. One of us?

JULIE. Not necessarily. But this next board.

LORNA. He'll select one of us then. Or both.

JULIE. I dug up somewhere in the correspondence that he's only allowed one.

LORNA. Secretarial?

JULIE. Possibly.

LORNA. Well, that's me gone if it is.

JULIE. Or just want an administrative. That's me gone.

Dirty mag?

(She picks up a magazine)

'Pretty Pelvis'.

(She giggles)

LORNA. Been lying around.

JULIE. Oscene. We have to pass judgement? This won't get through.

LORNA. No, it's too late - going back.

JULIE. Look at that - !

LORNA. K would pass anything. Depends on his mood.

JULIE. That's - no. I defy anyone to have a bust that size. It's not organic. K once said he liked dirty books. His tastes are very questionable, and I don't think that's a good idea in a censor.

LORNA. Would you call it suggestive?

JULIE. It's not natural. It's not like those... I mean, that - is simply overdeveloped.

LORNA. Ask K what he thinks of it.

JULIE. K needs a woman with personality. His marriage was his life's biggest mistake.

LORNA. Did you ever see his wife?

JULIE. Got an impression of her - quiet mousy thing. Terribly depressing. For him. The children are lovely, though. Gorgeous. They're baby angels.

LORNA. K adores children. He's an old sentimentalist.

JULIE. I may be pregnant.

LORNA. Really the pictures are the main point of these, but there's a ruling they have to have words: otherwise they come in a different category.

JULIE. I'm sick of these stories, they're pornographic. I'm going to do letters. Dear Mr Schmidt. I hate having to write to you, you obscene person.

(She hunts for her rubber)

Spelled his name wrong, I think. But it seems to be spelled two different ways anyway. I'll write love and kisses at the end. K is definitely the most boring man in the world. But he is... he does -

Give confidence.

He's a mature old bastard.

LORNA. One day Anna went to the front line of battle, to see her teacher, who had been fighting. All day Ann waited, listening to the sounds of battle.

In the evening her teacher was brought back on a stretcher - she had been badly wounded. Ann cried when she saw her - the face she had loved had been so disfigured - but the teacher was drugged and could feel little pain.

Later that night the others went away and Anna and her teacher were left together.

Anna spoke: the teacher answered. A few simple words was all she was capable of.

Then Anna wept. She climbed into the sleeping bag with her teacher, kissed and licked all her wounds - she caressed the bruised flesh and licked the blood from the body, tearing the bandages off until her teacher was naked. Then, hungrily, passionately, she

made love to her, and in doing this she felt both
solitude and anguish, since the teacher could not
respond. Only a trickle of saliva at the corner of the
mouth told her true tale.

JULIE. What?

LORNA. What?

JULIE. Told her what?

LORNA. Told her true tale.

JULIE. How obscene.

We regret we are unable, unavailable, unless,
useless...

LORNA. Style's not up to much.

JULIE. Need more coffee. Can't face this letter. I think I
know the man who it's to. Once met him at a party.
Case of only just.

LORNA. What was only just?

JULIE. Was as old as K, but - not married. Very suspect.
I like respectable married men best. You always know
where you stand with them. That's K's big advantage.
Children are also an advantage. I adore them and
adore those that have them.

LORNA. How old are K's children?

JULIE. This character tried to get me drunk. Indecent
performance. Jack had gone off to relieve himself and
this indecent character approached me. Eyes really
dirty, like an old pervert. His first remark was: 'I
like your appendages'. I said: 'I'll put you in the
obscene publications department. Bottom shelf.' I
won't tell you what he did next.

(She giggles)

Then Jack came back.

LORNA. I only have intellectual experiences at parties, usually with foreigners.

JULIE. Tell me about them. Do you like foreigners?

LORNA. Nothing to tell. Nothing ever happens.

JULIE. Why do you go to parties?

LORNA. Why?

JULIE. Mm...

LORNA. Obvious reason. I need a man.

JULIE. You mean you go on your own?

LORNA. I've thought it over. It's very simple. Without a man and without - you know... it's not that your life isn't complete, which is true in a way - it's just that you're missing something which nature intended you to have.

JULIE. I've got Jack. I could do without him.

LORNA. Yes. Yes, because you've got him. If you didn't you couldn't.

JULIE. Who says?

LORNA. It's physiological. I've decided I need a man from every point of view - emotionally, physically and mentally.

JULIE. They're not perfect you know, even Jack.

LORNA. Otherwise I'll rot.

JULIE. What a horrid idea.

LORNA. I don't mean organs atrophying and all that. It's just that I'll go bad inside and putrefy. I've thought it all out. I saw it all clearly this weekend.

JULIE. It sounds very depressing to me. Can't you find anyone then?

LORNA. That's what I was saying. I just don't.

JULIE. Why?

LORNA. I'm not attractive.

JULIE. You're very attractive. You're at least as attractive as me.

(Pause)

You just have your hair wrong.

LORNA. How should I have it?

JULIE. Well, should be blonde for a start. And you should smile. A good smile always warms the other person. It's a sort of message between you. 'Woman was made for man's pleasure' is the impression you want to give.

LORNA. Always comes out wrong. Sort of nervous grin. They back away in alarm. Then I just get all the leavings, foreigners and - not that I mind foreigners, really, they just want you to meet all their friends, rows and rows of idiotic friends, and families, interminable families, you all sit around feeling stupid.

JULIE. Never happened to me.

LORNA. Well, you select your men. Not all girls can. I can't.

JULIE. Sounds depressing. Not sure what you can do. But you know luck just suddenly changes. One day this, one day that. Actually I got beaten up by Jack last night.

LORNA. How nice.

JULIE. No, it was awful. He couldn't stop, went mad over something I said. Fists flying and so on. I was sure he'd kill me. In the end he just left, left me lying there in this pool of blood.

The strange thing was, after he'd gone I felt a sudden urge of love for him. Fantastic feeling - in the stomach you know. I just wanted him, wanted him, wanted him, to come back so we could make love.

LORNA. Did he?

JULIE. No, he didn't come, so then I began to hate him. In fact I hated him so much that I dreamed about Kernitz instead.

LORNA. Well, you're luckier than me.

JULIE. I often do. His children sometimes come into it. Once I dreamed they were whipping me. K looked on, smiling, then disappeared. Not a bad little dream.

Once I dreamed I was his wife.

I enjoyed that.

Mrs Kernitz.

Hope I'm not pregnant.

(A knock at the door. The girls sit down at their desks)

LORNA. Come in.

(FINN enters. He looks around uncertainly)

FINN. Kerniss.

LORNA. Can we help you?

FINN. I see Mr Kerniss.

LORNA. This is Mr Kernitz's office.

FINN. I see Mr Kerniss.

LORNA. You can't actually see him at the moment. He's not in the office. Do you wish to see Mr Kernitz?

FINN. Kerniss.

LORNA. Yes... You - have an appointment with him?

(FINN looks around him)

JULIE. I've got a phrase book somewhere.

(Some moments elapse)

LORNA. You're expecting Mr Kernitz for an interview? Interview?

FINN. Please?

LORNA. Well, Mr Kernitz isn't here at the moment. As you can see. He should be arriving fairly soon. Would you like to sit down?

FINN. I am waiting until Mr Kernitz.

LORNA. Sit down anyway. He ought to be here presently.

(FINN does not sit down, but continues to look uneasily about him)

FINN. I am seeing Mr Kerniss.

LORNA. We'll arrange that when he comes.

(Pause. Then, with a sudden effort)

FINN. So I explain, I come. Mr I am seeing. Waiting. He has tells me, I interview. I am coming for him.

JULIE. Gosh.

FINN. Please tell me if both I am at the right office for gentleman, also I ask do I have see the gentleman. I am not have seen the gentleman.

LORNA. We'll do what we can for you, naturally.

JULIE. Must have more coffee. Shouldn't you call him sir?

LORNA. Should I...?

JULIE. 'Scuse, anyway.

(She goes into the annexe. FINN remains stationary)

(Off, semi-audible) Plenty of water.

(She returns. To FINN)

JULIE. You have some coffee?

LORNA. Coffee, to drink.

JULIE. Yum, delicious. (Mimes)

FINN. Is good, I take.

LORNA. He takes.

(JULIE disappears)

Are you in censorship, or films?

(FINN looks at her for a while)

FINN. Yes.

JULIE. (Off) Milk?

LORNA. Mr Kernitz should be in, only, sometimes he's
liable to be later. Sometimes earlier, sometimes
later, you see? Variation.

Did you come far for your interview?

(JULIE returns with the coffee)

JULIE. Voici. Gave you a little milk because didn't catch your reply. Sugar lump if you're in the mood. In the saucer.

FINN. Maito.

JULIE. Not at all, sir.

I need this.

Ouch.

Thought you were Kernitz for a moment.

No one can do without coffee. I had such a dreadful night, you can't imagine. Fifth cup today, believe it or not. I don't suppose you do.

(FINN spills a little of his coffee into the saucer. Some falls onto the floor)

LORNA. Don't bother. We're leaving this place tomorrow as it is.

JULIE. I'll throw that away.

(She removes the saucer, dries the bottom of the cup, returns it to FINN and takes the saucer into the annexe)

FINN. I have appointment to see Mr Kerniss.

LORNA. You've come to the right place, anyway. Right office at least.

FINN. I have appointment.

LORNA. I thought you might.

(JULIE returns)

JULIE. Here you are. You can put it in it.

Would you like a roll? I mean, I hope actually you don't want one - there's only one left, for K, you see, but a biscuit... Like one of these?

FINN. Please?

LORNA. Get him the packet.

(JULIE brings him the packet and takes one out)

JULIE. They're good. They're coconut. Extra thin. Go
with coffee.

FINN. Thank you.

JULIE. Here.

(FINN stirs his coffee)

FINN. Hausköö.

JULIE. How much?

FINN. Hausköö.

JULIE. What-which?

FINN. Finn Hausköö.

(He indicates himself)

LORNA. Name.

Hausköö.

FINN. Hausköö.

LORNA. Julie.

Lorna.

Secretaries.

JULIE. Lorna's administrative assistant and I'm
secretary. More accurate.

FINN. Work here many year in office?

JULIE. One year.

FINN. Many paper, many book in office?

JULIE. Many book. It's our work.

We're leaving it all tomorrow.

All that blank-blank back to the manufacturers.

FINN. Is interesting.

LORNA. Is very interesting. Very dirty too, in fact.

(Some moments elapse)

FINN. Thank you coffee.

JULIE. Making it anyway. Keep awake. Lorna doesn't
drink it. Says it colours you brown inside.

LORNA. Do I?

JULIE. You did once, I'm positive.

(FINN picks up 'Pretty Pelvis'. He holds it up with an
expression of mingled interest and repugnance)

LORNA. Yes, that sort of thing.

(FINN reads)

What do you think of it?

JULIE. Any good? You like? I mean, it's dirty, isn't it?
No? Do you agree with me it's unnatural? Are you - I
mean, do you think men are attracted by that sort -
those sort of - those sort of poses? Which do you think
is the best one?

(FINN looks up with an odd smile)

FINN. Is interesting.

LORNA. We have to decide whether that sort of magazine is fit for people to read.

JULIE. Or look at.

LORNA. Or look at.

(FINN continues reading)

JULIE. Obviously gets something out of it.

Feeling depressed.

Keep thinking about yesterday. Trying to keep it at bay.

You see, what started it off: I went to see Jack in the evening, and there was this girl there. In his room. Undressed.

LORNA. Anything happening?

JULIE. Surprised she had the cheek to appear like that. She was fat. I didn't know what to do. I wished I'd made it up with Jack over the weekend. Perhaps I should have made the first move.

So there was this revolting nude bitch. Don't know how she dared parade herself like that.

LORNA. What was she like?

JULIE. I went straight out. Repulsive. Felt a bit peculiar. Went home. I suddenly thought - that was it. Finished. But our relationship was like a marriage. It was one really. The next thing was Jack came back - we had this row. I couldn't see why he'd done it you see.

(FINN puts the magazine down, rises and goes into the annexe)

LORNA. He given up?

JULIE. Probably checking on office equipment.

(FINN re-emerges)

Are you looking for something?

FINN. Please - gentleman convenience.

LORNA. I'll do it.

(She opens the door)

Follow.

(They both leave, and LORNA reappears a moment later. She sees some notes Finn has left on the arm of his chair)

LORNA. How is the character of the audience relevant to what are permitted to see?

JULIE. What's that?

LORNA. Does the sensitive of the old people prevent them to see or read certain works?

JULIE. I hope so.

LORNA. How far should the direct expression of sexuality permit?

JULIE. Are those the -

LORNA. Maybe meant for us to read.

JULIE. Should children be protected from sexual expressions? What does it mean?

LORNA. Sexual expressiveness, perhaps...

(FINN returns)

JULIE. Bonjour.

(Some moments elapse. FINN resumes his seat)

JULIE. Shall I take that - getting in your way?

(She takes his cup)

I'm sorry our leader hasn't arrived. Please accept our apology for him, sir.

LORNA. Don't be so formal. You'll scare him.

JULIE. Um - do you know how long your interview will be?

FINN. Please?

JULIE. How long?

FINN. In three days, then return.

JULIE. What?

FINN. I re-turn.

JULIE. If you're... If you're going to be quizzed by K we'd better warn you of some things. Presumably if you want the job. That is, he's not frightening, but you may find him, well, a bit off-putting at first.

LORNA. You may find him eccentric.

JULIE. Yes. Yes, he's -

LORNA. He knows the stuff and he -

JULIE. He's -

LORNA. He just has a curious way of putting it across, that is - you must be patient with him.

JULIE. He's terribly sweet, I mean, I love him and I'm sure Lorna does - though he's not exactly a young man - he's mature, you know.

LORNA. He's fifty something. Late fifties.

160

JULIE. Wife who's quite unsuitable. He needs someone with personality, you see.

LORNA. If you want him to respect your views don't say you believe in imposing ideas or directing taste - er -

FINN. Please?

LORNA. If you want to succeed - get the job - don't say you believe in forcing people to do anything.

JULIE. Be broadminded.

LORNA. Don't impose - say you don't want to -

JULIE. If he asks you to -

LORNA. - don't want to impose anything on anybody. Say you reflect, not direct the taste. Can you remember that? Reflect, not direct. It's the basic thing. In fact let him do most of the talking. It's safer.

JULIE. Ask him about himself - family, anything. He'll discuss that.

LORNA. Don't approve of authority - that is, don't approve of it too strongly, you can approve of it mildly. Say something like: 'I'm ready to listen to all points of view.' Can you remember that? You'll go down very well with that.

FINN. How long Mr Kerniss work in office?

LORNA. Here?

JULIE. One year.

FINN. He work one year?

LORNA. A bit less than a year. In this particular office.

FINN. I read you... I can read to you some question which later I am asking for Mr Kerniss.

(He picks up his notes)

LORNA. Yes...

FINN. I ask: now. First ; how is the character of the
audience relative to what they see?

JULIE. God.

LORNA. Something like - you have to consider the type
of audience - children, adults, old people. Each may
be sensitive to an area of - um - sorry, that's not
very neat. What I really mean is -

FINN. Also I ask - how far should the direct expression
of sexuality permit?

LORNA. How far should the direct expression of
sexuality be permitted? Well, it depends what you
mean by sexuality.

FINN. Please?

LORNA. I mean a child can be sexual - and also sexuality
can be sanctioned by society - that is consecrated by
marriage or ensomethinged by society when outside
marriage.

Now inside marriage you may think it's consecrated
and therefore you should not represent it - the trouble
being that if you don't you leave blanks which
imagination may fill, and -

outside marriage you may say there are those who
feel it should not be represented, since to represent
it may encourage it.

Of course, it's more complicated - ,

Kernitz's view seems to be - as far as you can say he
has a view - that nothing should be kept from the child.
Do you follow this?

FINN. I say so Mr Kerniss.

LORNA. No - this - what I said was K's view - those last things. You must say - or should say - for instance - something vague and flexible, i.e. the child should be allowed to find his own path, dirty or clean, that's to say dirty books should not be put out of his reach.

FINN. Dirty book?

LORNA. Yes, you know: immoral books.

JULIE. Tell us a bit about yourself: we're always interested in the personal side. Are you married, for instance? If it isn't rude to enquire.

FINN. Married?

(Some moments elapse)

- yes -

JULIE. How did you meet your wife? I mean to say -

FINN. Not married.

LORNA. You're not married?

JULIE. I thought you said you were.

LORNA. Are you married? Do you have a wife?

FINN. Wife?

- no -

JULIE. Oh, well: do you have any - er -

LORNA. Mistresses...

JULIE. Shh - girlfriends - ?

(FINN does not reply)

Don't be shy. You can tell us.

We're censors.

Tell us about your girlfriends. Do you enjoy having them?

FINN. Please?

JULIE. Girlfriends.

FINN. Friend of girl? Girl who is friend?

JULIE. Yes: girlfriends.

FINN. Sepa ymmarrettara oire.

LORNA. You're bewildering him.

FINN. Ymmarrettara.

JULIE. It's all right. Sorry.

FINN. Oire sepa friend of girl, parveketta hausköö girl who is friend.

LORNA. Yes. Um.

JULIE. He's peculiar.

I'm going to finish these.

Dear Sir.

How do you spell 'incurred'?

(KERNITZ enters)

KERNITZ. Police just broke up a children's brothel.

JULIE. Morning Mr Kernitz.

KERNITZ. Youngest child seven years old.

JULIE. I'll get your coffee.

KERNITZ. Nuisance, this kind of thing, isn't it? Young children on the streets... organised prostitution.

LORNA. Could you - sorry - could you just initial these two? Overdue.

KERNITZ. Here?

Oh, yes.

(He signs. LORNA takes the sheets, puts them in envelopes, etc.)

So what happens, of course? Same old problem, isn't it? Soon as any sort of... moral racket, like this... comes to light - going to hit the same reaction. Section of the public calling it our responsibility.

LORNA. Who was organising it?

KERNITZ. (To FINN) Good morning. How are you?

(To LORNA) No, usual thing... a million editorials... keep the public's nose out of the dirt... moral scandals like this won't occur. They honestly believe that: they honestly do.

LORNA. Who was organising this brothel?

KERNITZ. Young children.

LORNA. Just - the children themselves?

KERNITZ. Children, children, right down the line. Boss only about nine years old, so far as I could see.

These kids... were selling themselves.

(JULIE returns with coffee, and gives it to him)

JULIE. Here's your coffee, Mr Kernitz.

KERNITZ. To members of the public. And the public were taking them at their word.

165

Now, you know, these kids... had probably never seen a pornographic book in their lives.

JULIE. Hope it's all right.

KERNITZ. Thanks, Julie. Couldn't even read, I dare say.

JULIE. You're welcome.

LORNA. That's Mr Hausköö.

KERNITZ. Mr -

LORNA. Hausköö, I think. Finn Hausköö.

FINN. Finn Hausköö. Finn Hausköö.

KERNITZ. Call you Finn. I'm Kernitz. In charge of the depot. Do... take a seat.

(Some moments elapse)

Yes... quite a scene. Press haven't got to it yet. They're still... police still quizzing these innocent little creatures.

LORNA. What are they like?

KERNITZ. Little beauties... tiny little creatures. There they are... getting their grilling like the boy in the picture. 'When did you last...?' Some of those nippers hardly have the power of speech. Beautiful little kiddies, though. Like to ask him to sit down, Lorna?

LORNA. Please sit down, Mr Hausköö.

(FINN does not sit)

KERNITZ. May sound unbelievable. I couldn't get an ear to it at first, myself. Getting old, I suppose, evidently. Left behind by the stream of events.

What do you think of it, Finn? Shocking stuff, no?

166

(To LORNA, about material he has had in his hand for a while)

Er... two of these are returnable. I see they... two wasted. B & D. Both on top.

LORNA. What's your attitude to it?

KERNITZ. My...? Shocked... shocked... shocked like everybody else, of course. The point is, you see... this type of scandal erupting, a good number of fingers are going to start pointing in a number of directions, aren't they?

LORNA. At you?

KERNITZ. Well, that's one direction, isn't it?... Vociferous elements. Hysteria. Demands made. Well, it is a moral issue, isn't it? Trouble is, whose? No one knows. That's when the finger starts pointing.

JULIE. Hope your coffee's all right, Mr Kernitz.

(She is writing)

KERNITZ. Of course, we... we merely reflect, we can't direct the taste. Very good, thank you. We do, we do reflect, don't we, Finn... don't you think? Do you have a view here at all?

LORNA. His English is not very strong.

JULIE. If you explain - a sign helps.

KERNITZ. Well, Finn... interview required, that it?

(Some moments elapse)

FINN. Interview.

KERNITZ. Understands me, at least. What have you girls been confusing him with? Right. (To FINN) If you can just count your chickens for a few moments I shall be at your service. Thing or two to run through with me girls.

LORNA. Oh, this arrived this morning.

KERNITZ. Title?

LORNA. 'Artes Amoris'.

KERNITZ. Amatory arts. Any good?

LORNA. I've only read a few pages here and there.

JULIE. It's very dirty.

KERNITZ. What, obscene publication?

JULIE. It's crude, you know. Not what they say, the way they put it.

KERNITZ. Hm. Pose any problems?

LORNA. Most of it's psychology - psychology of women.

KERNITZ. Seem to ring true at all?

LORNA. Don't know. It's written by a man. I think it's overspecific.

KERNITZ. Read me a section which you think is over-specific.

How long are they giving us?

LORNA. Two weeks. Here's some.

'Of the two sexes the woman is basically the stronger. Closer to nature and the force of propagation she will use any methods to mate successfully with a series of partners. She seeks to absorb and possess the male, but this intensity can conflict with her need for a variety of partners, since variety ensures her best chance of fertility. '

KERNITZ. No comment.

LORNA. 'Man is governed by theoretical application of principle. Woman is amoral since she will follow a code only if her feelings correspond with the code. She is beyond morality.'

KERNITZ. Julie, any views? Are you beyond morality?

JULIE. (Shrugs)

KERNITZ. Do you agree with it?

JULIE. I don't understand it.

KERNITZ. Lorna?

LORNA. I don't know what to think of it. I'm not sure. I don't think you can classify women.

Most of it, after the psychology part or whatever, is just a description of lovemaking technique.

KERNITZ. I'll give it an eyeing.

(LORNA puts the book on the table for him)

JULIE. Is Jimmy better?

KERNITZ. Run right into another bug, little stinker.

JULIE. Poor thing.

KERNITZ. Finishes with flu, comes out with whooping cough.

LORNA. That's the youngest, isn't it?

KERNITZ. Five on Friday. Now he'll have to celebrate in bed.

Well... I'm keeping our young friend waiting.

Buried in a book.

Well, Finn, shall we have our little discussion?

(To LORNA) You might look through these while we're talking. All checked, I think. Might make sure.

LORNA. Right.

(She goes into the annexe)

JULIE. I'll just take this.

(She takes KERNITZ's cup and leaves with a smile)

KERNITZ. All right, Julie.

(He tidies up a few papers, nods cheerfully to FINN)

Seat? Less formal.

(FINN sits)

Here we are.

(He sits down himself)

Now... anything you'd like to ask me, or tell me, first?

No? No?

Lights aren't too bright for you, are they? I could adjust the -

FINN. Please?

KERNITZ. Not too bright... bright, in the eye?

FINN. Not - ...

KERNITZ. Well. What to discuss then.

Note you're having a peek at 'Pretty Pelvis'.

What do you think of it?

Any views?

170

Good magazine?

FINN. Is interesting.

KERNITZ. What about the colour - ?

FINN. Yes...

KERNITZ. The nudes. Happy with them?

Feel, do you, they expose too much...

... of their bodies?

FINN. (With difficulty) I think you can control the amount of body showing.

KERNITZ. You control it. I see. Now, let's consider what happens to the individual when he reads this magazine. The individual - very important person - much neglected. Now what happens to him - what happens to you - when you read a copy?

FINN. I think... is disgusting... a copy.

KERNITZ. It disgusts you. Is there any... pleasure mingling with the disgust?

FINN. Please?

KERNITZ. You take no... enjoyment at all in reading this magazine.

FINN. I am disgusted the copy.

Pictures disgust. Is no careful -

(Some moments elapse)

KERNITZ. Is - ?

FINN. Is no -

(Some moments elapse)

Is no - is not crude the -

(Some moments elapse)

KERNITZ. The pictures are not crude?

FINN. Are crude - are crude the -

(Some moments elapse)

KERNITZ. Well, we might leave that one for the moment.

Now, imagine instead that you have to judge as a parent. What do you do if you are a parent, and your daughter wished to read it?

FINN. Daughter - ?

KERNITZ. Wished to read it. I mean, you may not be married, you may not have a daughter - but, if you did... would you allow her to read it?

FINN. (Baffled) I have not daughter... I read to daughter?

KERNITS. No... Would you permit, would you allow a young girl to read it?

FINN. I don't let.

KERNITZ. I see. Why not?

FINN. (Passionately) Is too young!

KERNITZ. I see. How will it affect her if she reads it?

FINN. Hirveä.

KERNITZ. I beg your pardon?

FINN. Likuttaa kehno pikakirjoittajatar. Poikkeuksetta.

KERNITZ. I'm not with you.

(Pause)

FINN. Hirveä.

(Some moments elapse)

KERNITZ. I had no wish to sound aggressive. My intention,
you see, is to discuss with you... find out your ideas,
views, nothing more than that.

There's no need to answer at once... think about it,
and if you choose to answer, you can.

We'll try something more general, shall we?

All right?

Try this one, then.

When did you first wish to become a censor?

(Some moments elapse)

FINN. When I see a country...

The country...

(A painful silence)

Low moral.

KERNITZ. Bravo, the low morals of the country. Well,
I agree. We all agree. Morality does seem lower than
it was, doesn't it?

Next question - what do we do about it? How do we
correct this... low morality?

Take time over this one.

(Fifteen seconds elapse)

That's right, take your time.

(Ten seconds elapse)

Don't rush into an answer.

FINN. An answer...

KERNITZ. Don't rush into one.

(Pause)

FINN. I think you keep standard high with reflecting taste of the people, no directing. Reflect, no direct.

KERNITZ. Well put... yes. Yes. I like that.

FINN. (Has no more to say) Is my idea.

KERNITZ. Good.

Now, we were talking earlier about this junior brothel. Now... what would you... how would you deal... with such a question?

Supposing it came up.

FINN. Brothel.... of children.

KERNITZ. Yes, yes. Yes, yes, yes.

FINN. I close. Close it.

KERNITZ. Close it down. I see.

FINN. I close.

KERNITZ. Yes, but - the public. This is where the question may loom, may it not?

Some one challanges your position, suggests... you follow me... that it is due to you - your own work, as censor, that this sort of... social... stigma... arises.

There's an attempt to displace you.

What do you do then?

FINN. Now I ask you question? Not?

KERNITZ. Er - I thought you were answering mine, but still...

Go ahead.

FINN. How is character of audience relative to what they see?

KERNITZ. How... hmm. Well, if I'm right in interpreting your question, you are discussing audience. Whether one should limit the sale of a book, is that it?

FINN. How far - I ask this - how far should the direct expression of sexuality permit?

KERNITZ. Another question. Well, perhaps a fair one. In answering it, you should consider what you mean by 'expression'. For example, if I make love to my wife I am expressing my sexuality. But if I have intercourse with a prostitute, or even an animal, I may still be expressing sexuality.

Now, how far this type of sexuality - you might break it down into legitimate and illegitimate - should be presented on a screen, say. Should a child, that is, see me in the act of love with my wife?

FINN. A child?

KERNITZ. Yes.

FINN. Act of love?

KERNITZ. Yes, act of love.

FINN. My wife?

KERNITZ. My wife.

FINN. (With increasing alarm and disbelief) My wife?

KERNITZ. Well - your wife, or my wife.

FINN. (Deeply shocked) Is terrible.

KERNITZ. Yes, I see.

FINN. Is terrible.

KERNITZ. Yes, I see. You're shocked. So am I. Private is not the same as public. We're both agreed.

But where do we go from there? We're censors, not members of the public.

FINN. (Somewhat uncertainly) Where go from there?

KERNITZ. Where indeed?

FINN. (Following up tentatively) Where from there indeed?

KERNITZ. You tell me. What next move do you take?

FINN. (Apparently horrified) Where? Where? Kyllastyn hukka huolitellusti, opinto pudota, tarkastele laake.

KERNITZ. I don't understand all of that.

FINN. Tarkastele kummastun lauta jannittaa, kai kyyristyn nakoinen.

KERNITZ. I see.

FINN. Mutisi on jano.

KERNITZ. Well, I'm sorry. Perhaps the question offended you.

One thing, now. I have it here, on this paper you sent me.

I asked you how you would go about things if you were in charge of this department.

You wrote - I have it here - 'radical changes, a different approach to the problems'. Radical changes. What sort of changes would you make?

(Some moments elapse)

What would you change?

If you want a change, you must feel that something - this or that - is unsatisfactory.

(Some moments elapse. FINN clears his throat)

You can't approve of the situation altogether, since you say - I have it here before me - that you will wish to make changes.

What sort of changes?

FINN. (Still terrified) Kavelypuku! Menetella vesivoima, syrja karhu kaltainen.

KERNITZ. I'm sorry. You understand that though I don't wish to rush you, to make you say something you might wish to revoke later, I must, obviously, get something down. Something about you. I must distinguish you by one or two statements. Those which I feel represent you.

FINN. Menettelen kiinostua. Makua.

(He takes a biscuit out of his pocket and begins to eat it)

KERNITZ. This becomes a problem for me. I must ask you to make some remarks which are comprehensible to me.

(FINN continues to eat)

Perhaps you'd like to write them on this sheet of paper.

(He gets up and hands FINN a piece of paper and a pencil. FINN backs in terror)

FINN. Ilme vahingoittaa!

KERNITZ. No, no. That's all right.

FINN. Minun taytyy!

KERNITZ. Please take your seat again.

(FINN shrieks with terror, standing behind his chair for protection)

FINN. Taytyy!

KERNITZ. No, no, no.

(He sits down.

FINN squats down behind his chair and shouts at him)

FINN. Sairistui valitettavasti toire, tasmalleen, siksi sisalto - tiomeen senttimetri tasku vaara vaalalinen.

(Some moments elapse)

KERNITZ. Now, Finn, I'm not sure what has disturbed you. If you would like to sit down again, you can tell me, at your leisure, what you would like to.

FINN. Kenties.

KERNITZ. You might like a cup of coffee.

(He presses a bell. JULIE appears)

JULIE. Mr Kernitz?

FINN. Voileipa... nautinto!

(He goes out)

KERNITZ. Couldn't wait, I'm afraid.

JULIE. Something upset him?

KERNITZ. Problem.

JULIE. He was funny. We couldn't understand him.

KERNITZ. Difficult customer, yes.

JULIE. Would you like me to go after him? I could try...
ready to rush out - .

KERNITZ. In his present mood I can't see it would be much
use.

JULIE. Do you want me to write a report?

KERNITZ. We'll leave that till later.

JULIE. Anything else?

KERNITZ. Letters.

I want you to write - I'll leave you to write the letter -
to a man who -

(Some moments elapse.

JULIE sits with pencil in hand)

KERNITZ. ... has recently completed his book, 'A
Dictionary of Morality'.

I have the proofs of this. His name escapes me - something grotesque. You'll find him in the correspondence
under 'Local Licensing Committee'.

Now, the sense is this. I don't believe the public is
ready for his book. I have no power to prevent him
publishing it, in this case, but I would like him to
reconsider his material.

The moral attitude of the book is at fault: it sees
morality as a prejudged issue and attempts to define
it.

He writes: 'The aim of morality is to enhance the life
of the individual - ' ... something like that. He feels
that present-day morality, such as it is, is misleading...

Anyway, you know my views - put it in your own words,

and sign my name at the bottom.

JULIE. Yes. All right, Mr Kernitz.

(She completes her notes)

Any other letters?

KERNITZ. No.

You can go if you wish.

JULIE. If that's all.

(She gets up and picks up one or two personal possessions. She puts on her coat)

Might come back tomorrow and send off the last few things.

Right then.

Goodbye.

(She pauses at the door)

KERNITZ. Incidentally: - you might like to come round and help look after the kids tonight. Give them their tea. Watch television.

Their mother's in hospital.

JULIE. I'd love to, Mr Kernitz.

KERNITZ. Seven o'clock.

JULIE. All right.

Bye then.

(She goes)

LORNA. Anything for me to do now?

KERNITZ. There's a little winding up I'd like you to do.

Synopsis files.

(LORNA goes to the cabinet, unlocks a drawer, opens it, takes out a number of files and puts them on the table.

She looks at KERNITZ.

Some moments elapse)

Pending. Under... Historical.

(LORNA opens the appropriate file.

She looks at KERNITZ)

The film is called 'The Commune', I think.

LORNA. Yes.

KERNITZ. Can you read me out the synopsis given there?

LORNA. A girl, Juliet, is wounded in battle. Her teacher is behind the lines. Juliet's body is brought home on a stretcher.

Juliet is conscious but drowsy: she says 'hello' to the teacher. The teacher (Mrs Groat) takes off Juliet's clothes, cutting the -

(She turns over the page)

material where necessary. She then bathes the wounds. Juliet cries and clutches the side of the stretcher to avoid the pain.

The teacher falls in love with Juliet. At night she strips off her own clothes and embraces Juliet, kissing and licking her wounds. The two women kiss and bite each other.

(She looks up at KERNITZ)

KERNITZ. Could you read me the objections sent in by the 'Protect the Public' group?

LORNA. 'We feel that the film degrades womanhood. It indulges the common childish fantasy where the young child idolises the teacher in a quasi-sexual way and dreams of being hurt and caressed by the teacher. That a girl at the start of her emotional teens should dream this, is one thing; that it should be portrayed, and that the teacher should be so far abased as to shame herself in front of the pupil, is both unnecessary and in bad taste. Any person will enjoy the film: equally their values will be lowered and perverted by it. Discipline, always a renunciation, will be foregone, authority will be spurned. Ordinary restraints will disappear and humanity burn in St. Augustine's cauldron of impure loves. Save our youth from this plight. '

KERNITZ. Our remarks.

LORNA. Our remarks: the objection is upheld: the film is a fantasy and is... banned.

Six months later we repealed it, the film was shown to a selected audience, and three weeks after that to full audiences.

KERNITZ. Do you think it corrupted the kiddies?

LORNA. I doubt if they understood it.

KERNITZ. What about the teenagers?

LORNA. We have only one record here - that's of a teeager that liked it.

KERNITS. What did she say?

LORNA. It was a boy. He wrote: 'I liked the film because it showed my teacher behaving like a natural woman. '

KERNITZ. Ah.

LORNA. He went on: 'I prefer films about men because I

182

like heroism and warfare - especially where the camera gets caught up in gunfire. '

KERNITZ. Gunfire? What does he mean by that?

LORNA. I suppose he means where it whirls around, as in 'Southern Steps', you know, when he dies the camera spins round, showing the trees and the enemy tank.

(Some moments elapse)

That sort of thing.

KERNITS. I've only known one person die. At my age, I should imagine this is rare. It was my mother's mother. She was very seriously ill - as they say - had an unnameable disease that was, quite literally, eating away her insides.

Day by day there was less of her.

It was similar to a film of a growing child shown backwards. She seemed to be approaching the womb each day, became more and more like a foetus.

As a spectacle I think it was more disgusting than any dirty film. And no censor could prevent me, or those in the same ward, seeing it. I believe a great poet died in the same manner.

This was the visual aspect. As for the sound-track... well, that was worse.

The woman - though very thin, unrecognisably thin - retained the full power of her voice, and she screamed day and night until her vocal cords had quite gone, and then she made a rasping sound. She kept this up. I suspect it was that part of her brain was involved, and that not all the screaming was due to pain. I prefer to think that.

She didn't die, she lived amazingly: each day her continuing existence was a miracle as remarkable as sunrise ; and her pain, too, seemed miraculous - her hair turned white.

When she died, I cried in my wife's arms. For two years afterwards I hated the sound of the human voice.

LORNA. Make love to me.

KERNITZ. Whenever she stopped screaming, she vomited.

LORNA. Make love to me now.

KERNITZ. I'm sorry - ?

LORNA. Sleep with me.

(Some moments elapse. He looks at her)

KERNITZ. Are you all right?

LORNA. Make love to me, please, on the chair, on the floor, anywhere.

Please.

(KERNITZ walks over to her. He puts his arm on her shoulder. She remains very still. He pats her shoulder, not quite knowing what to say. He looks at her for a moment or two)

KERNITZ. Now.

You look after yourself.

You've been overworking.

(Pause)

You go home and have a rest.

LORNA. Kernitz. I love you. I want to sleep with you. I have to, and you have to. We must sleep together. I want you to make love to me. I want you to do that with me.

KERNITZ. Can you stow the files, Lorna, lock up the
    cabinet, then the room, and leave the keys below, all
    right?

    (Some moments elapse)

LORNA. All right.

    (KERNITZ collects his coat. He goes into the annexe
    and returns with a glass of water, which he puts in
    LORNA's hand. He pats her shoulder again, and goes.

    LORNA remains standing motionless in the room.
    Presently she goes to a chair and sits down.

    After a while she rises, goes to the window and opens
    it.

    She looks out.

    There is a knock at the door.

    She pauses.

    Another knock)

LORNA. What?

    (FINN enters)

FINN. I am to speak Kerniss.

LORNA. What? Gone. He's gone.

FINN. Come to say apologise for leaving interview, sorry
    for behaviour was hasty and he will forgive and continue,
    will talk.

LORNA. He isn't here.

FINN. Here?

LORNA. Isn't here.

FINN. Is coming?

(Some moments elapse)

LORNA. He's unlikely to come.

When he goes for the day he doesn't come back. He - it's not his practice.

FINN. He will speak.

LORNA. He won't speak here, John.

He has gone home.

FINN. But for the talk?

LORNA. You spoiled your chance for that, didn't you?

FINN. Please?

LORNA. Nerves, I suppose. I suppose you were nervous. Jul and I heard most of it. I was sorry for you. K's methods don't always put people at their ease.

Perhaps you were just... ill-suited to one another.

FINN. Mr Kerniss has not often spoken to the people.

LORNA. I don't know what you mean, John.

It sounds promising. Oh, God.

(She sits down)

I feel sick. It may be your nerves were on edge, and with some people this - you know - puts them off. They're all right when they're not on edge. When they are, they... just can't say a single right thing.

Anyway if you'd found some simple way of calming your nerves down before that you might have got through that.

But then you'd have taken the job off us.

You can relax now. I'm a girl, but that doesn't mean
I'm going to hurt you.

Jul and K will soon be in each other's arms, I suppose,
watching telly.

They'll make love in the presence of the kids.

If you'd like to sit down I'll explain what might -

(She gets up and puts the files away)

- help with any future occasion. Seeing Kernitz or
anybody.

There's a chair.

You have to sit. Otherwise I can't go on.

There.

(She moves the chair, and indicates it.

Finn sits down)

Thank you.

This is called relaxation. Several activities have - .
With several activities, relaxation is the first, is the
most important thing. Relates to your nervous system
and your nervous system to your head and thoughts and
feelings.

First you have to be conscious of limbs and of every
muscle. Do this by... tensing them a bit first.

Hold out your hands.

(She holds out her own hands.

FINN does not reciprocate, so she puts out his hands
for him)

Now tense your palm.

Make it go hard. Concentrate it.

Relax it.

Now again hard.

Relax.

Again.

Relax.

This locates the muscles. All right? Makes you conscious of them.

Consciousness is necessary so you can relax all of them.

Clench fist.

(She does this, and helps FINN to clench his)

Forward side now.

(She performs this exercise, also helping FINN)

Locates wrist: you see the muscle, the feeling is in the wrist. You relax it.

Now arm. Arm at the front.

I'll explain you the reason for this. If you're tense you're prepared for action. And action means concentrate. On one thing - one reason - and blot out several others. Thoughts are all strangled if you're tense.

If your thoughts are free, and untense, you're in a much better position to do what you want.

FINN. I find it is difficult to speak Kerniss because are not listen you speech. You speak, he speak, alltime he... he not...

LORNA. - Doesn't take in what you say. Yes. I think that
may be sometimes true. Sometimes he doesn't appear
to.

Intelligent person, of course.

But sometimes I think he's a terrible egoist, and
terribly immoral, just disgustingly, worse than a
little child burning a cat, or anything similar.

FINN. He talk - is not listen.

LORNA. Perhaps, I mean, quite likely.

FINN. In my home - my country - always is person
interested. He give coffee, he ask what news, you talk,
you tell him news of next village, who die, who have
child - you tell him what you learn and things that
happen in village.

LORNA. Make love to me.

FINN. Please?

LORNA. Make love to me.

FINN. Kekö.

LORNA. Please do it. I want you to do it. Make love to
me. On the chair. On the floor. Anywhere. I must.
You must. You want to.

FINN. Kenties laatikkoa siipi kauhea!

LORNA. Make love to me. Do it to me.

To me.

189

APPENDIX

(This appendix contains production notes for JENS)

In JENS the HORSE and HEN were originally envisaged as wearing full animal costume (perhaps with the exception of the head), but not possessing animal characteristics.

BIRGER is pronounced 'beer - ya'.

In production, realistic style and speed is advisable for JENS (as for all three plays in this volume). However, in the first production of JENS, certain stylised groupings were used sparingly, by way of contrast to an otherwise realistic treatment. I give examples of two such passages, as originally performed.

*

(JENS. page 86)

TEACHER. Thank you.

> (She accepts an orange from BRAATOY.
>
> The following grouping occurs, characters involved sitting cross-legged on the floor:

LORETTE		HORSE
ING-BRITT	SANDIE	BIRGER)

TEACHER. The meeting -

> The blind - you know the blind young fellow - freckles - plays a flute, I believe -
>
> D'you have a knife for this?

PEART. I'll - yes - just - .

TEACHER. A knife. Yes. I -

This fellow was put into a competition - won it -
probably through default.

They gave him a cello.

(The HORSE rises. The entire group - as previous
page - rise simultaneously)

HORSE. Yes. I - I was glad to hear you say that. I was
present at the meeting, actually, and notified - noted
the - this - , and -

Actually I was puzzled by the gift of a cello. Can he
play?

TEACHER. I don't know if he's musical. Most of the
children, of course, are taught rudiments. And one
comes across adults who listen - hiding themslves
away - try and capture hints taught to the children.

HORSE. No, he couldn't play. This what stranged the
encounter.

PEART. Blunt one.

HORSE. He was given the cellist - the cello.

(The HORSE sits. Group ditto)

TEACHER. I never heard what he did with it. Didn't -
didn't seem to know what it was for.

PEART. I'll try that. Give me the cutter.

TEACHER. He understood the meaning of the gift.

(HORSE and group rise)

HORSE. But that's not enough for most of us to understand
what he meant. Let me try to explain: if I write an
account, I have to clarify the scene - I take events -
you and I do...

(HORSE and group take one pace backwards and stop)

HORSE. But events by themselves are events.

(The group sits. HORSE remains standing)

BRAATOY. Could you distract him a little, Birger, with some object?

*

(JENS: page 94)

HORSE. Is there something there that might interest me?

(Grouping:

ING-BRITT   LOUYS   BIRGER   HORSE   SANDIE

standing in a straight line, facing left)

SANDIE. Probably an old woodland design - or might be abstract.

(LOUYS sets it down, returns to his place in line. Group does a left turn, to face audience)

HORSE. Come to think of it, might be something I could help to clarify.

(Group left-turns again, to face right)

ING-BRITT. Can you take charge of the horse? I don't want him to intrude if it can be avoided.

(A final left-turn, to leave group all with backs to audience)

BIRGER. Come on, Matthew, I'll show you a new game.

(Grouping and movement revert to normal)

HORSE. Always glad to break fresh ground, Birger.

This book is to ' 　 on or bef
　　the ' 　　　 below

fore